YOUR
Simple Home
HANDBOOK

30 projects to help your home breathe

By Elsie Callender
RichlyRooted.com

Copyright © 2015 by Elsie Callender

Formatting and cover design by Margaret Anne Darazs of NaturalChow.com

Formatted for print by SimplyDesigns.org

All Rights Reserved. No part of this document or the related links may be reproduced or redistributed in any form, by any means (electronic, photocopying, or otherwise) without the prior written permission of the author.

This book is dedicated to Eric, my husband and best friend. I love making a home with you!

Special thanks to Mom, Dad, and Emma for their input about various sections of this book. Thank you also to my dear blogging friends, for your daily encouragement as we blog together, and your excitement about this endeavor! Thank you Margaret Anne, for making this book beautiful. And to Erin Odom, for being a teacher and kindred spirit.

TABLE OF CONTENTS

Introduction 6
Chapter 1: Bedroom 15
    Wardrobe.. 16
    Shoes... 23
    Accessories 29
    Inside Your Purse 33
    Nightstand.. 35
Chapter 2: Bathroom 37
    Bathroom Cabinets............................. 38
    Makeup 42
    Shower 45
    Medicine Cabinet................................ 47
Chapter 3: Kitchen.................................... 49
    Kitchen Counters................................ 50
    Kitchen Cabinets 53
    Utensil Drawer 56
    Dishes 58
    Dining Room 61
Chapter 4: Housekeeping 64
    Cleaning Supplies 65
    Laundry Room 68
    Linen Closet... 72
Chapter 5: Children 76
    Kids' Toys 77
    Kids' Clothes 80
Chapter 6: Entertainment 82
    Keepsakes 83
    Crafts and Hobbies............................. 88
    Games 92
    Books 95
    Media 101

Chapter 7: Work 103
    Desk 104
    Paper 107
Chapter 8: The Edges 111
    Attic 112
    Coat Closet 115
    Entryway 117
    Car 119
Getting Your Stuff Out The Door 121
Conclusion 125
About the Author 127
Simple Home Checklist 128

INTRODUCTION

This book is for all the people who are tired of too much stuff. It's for those who want to cut the clutter and actually use and enjoy what they own. It's for people who want to craft a beautiful, inviting home without spending a penny. This book is for people who recognize that "more" doesn't always mean "better" and who are willing to be a little counter-cultural for the sake of breathing space in their home.

If you want to be intentional about how you steward your possessions and how you design your living space, this book is for you.

My Journey to Simple Living

Growing up, I accumulated far, far more items than any little girl needs or could ever use. I would keep stuff for the inherent value that I perceived it had, rather than for its usefulness to me. I think some of my tendency to hang on to stuff was due to the fact that I had five siblings. I found that my possessions could help to define my personality and interests, setting me apart from my siblings and what they had (no one else owned a miniature accordion, for instance!).

My view of stuff took a radical shift when my family moved to the mission field when I was in high school. We flew to Costa Rica, ready to spend three months at language school with only as much as our suitcases could hold. The house we rented was furnished, but we had to bring down our own bedding, kitchen utensils, and school supplies, which left just a little space for clothes and any other accessories or entertainment we wanted to take with us.

As three months turned into ten, we became increasingly resourceful with our meager wardrobes and household goods. And during this time I realized two very important truths:

1. I didn't need much to get by
2. I valued the stuff I did have more

They were important lessons, but it would take a few more years for them to really sink in. While we were in Costa Rica, and later on the mission field in Chile, we stored the bulk of our possessions back home in the United States. Everything was waiting for us when we returned, and although much of it was a burden to come back to, we settled in all too easily to the habit of owning too much stuff.

In college I got more practice detaching from my belongings, but I never made a long term commitment to living with less. While I was very selective about the items I brought with me for the school year, the bulk of my possessions were waiting to confront me when I returned home each summer.

I had another living-out-of-a-suitcase experience when I studied abroad in Oxford for a semester. It was my first taste of true minimalism. I fit all my books, clothes, shoes, and accessories into one suitcase, and I realized I didn't need much at all to survive. I enjoyed the freedom of so few items. Picking out clothes each day was a breeze—I rotated through the same pieces every week, then washed them and repeated the process. I bought a new scarf, a T-shirt, and a dress during my time there, but other than that—I had plenty! I had three pairs of shoes, one framed picture for my desk, my journal, a camera, and a small stack of books that I needed for the semester.

My self-imposed minimalism was the perfect match for those months of my life. I had less stuff but more breathing room. It was easy to keep my room neat, and with fewer distractions and less choices I was able to focus my efforts on the grueling academic schedule—while also finding time to breathe in the city.

That spring, the freedom of less made me wonder: What if I could capture this way of life permanently? What if I could strip away the clutter—and the stress that comes with it—and enjoy more breathing room in my life and in my home?

The truth is, I'm not really a minimalist, and ultimately that's not my goal. But a girl who wants a simple life? That's me. I don't want to always live out of a suitcase (although I'm up for adventures!) but I do want to be intentional about the things I own. I want to offload my excess and be honest about what's truly important to me and to my home.

For me, it took this sequence of experiments of living with less to realize that I could make it a lifelong habit. Through college and after, I pared down on my stuff box by box, hoping to reach a point where I was truly satisfied with the amount of things I owned. But it wasn't enough. After I returned to my home turf, it was back to the same old stuff. I went through a box here or there and each season I would donate a few clothing items, but my efforts never made much of a difference. I still had plenty to take with me when I got married.

As I moved my stuff from apartment to apartment in the first four years of our marriage, I was frequently confronted with just how much clutter I'd brought into the relationship. My desire to simplify reached a peak, and finally I launched a series about simplifying on my blog to document my journey and share ideas with my readers.

Before our most recent move to a 600 square-foot cabin in Alabama, my husband caught the simplifying bug, too, and together we worked through each area of our home, examining everything from furniture to kitchen utensils as we decided what we really needed to take with us.

Our little cabin lacks a few things like closets, a pantry, kitchen drawers, and significant wall space. We couldn't have fit into this size home unless we'd really gotten serious about purging. Previously, our *modus operandi* when it came to simplifying was to scan a box or pile of stuff and ask: "What can I pull out? What can I get rid of?" We'd select a few items to take to Goodwill, and call it done. But in preparation for our move **we examined every single item** we owned with a critical eye, mentally interrogating it with the following questions:

- **Does this fit with the style of our new home?**
- **Do we already have one?**
- **Do we use this a lot? Is this worth taking up space for the amount of use or kind of use this item gets?**
- **Do we love it?**
- **Would we miss this item if it were gone?**
- **Can we do without this item?**

We ended up having a lot less than we began with, and while our home feels snug and full (because, after all, it is still just a 600 foot cabin with limited storage space), it still feels breathable.

Of course, there's always more we can get rid of, and keeping our lives simple requires ongoing maintenance. But it feels good to have arrived in many ways, too. We've had a breakthrough, and now we're enjoying the benefits of a simple home.

Your Journey to Simple Living

You're probably reading this book because you're interested in simple living on some level. Maybe you need some more motivation to tackle the clutter which has a strangle hold on your home. **Consider these ten reasons to get serious about simplifying your living space:**

1. Simplifying your stuff is energizing, addictive, and fun—once you start, you'll want to keep going.
2. Getting rid of stuff you don't need or care about will help you have a more beautiful, peaceful home.
3. Purging loosens your grip on material possessions.
4. When you purge, you discover what you own (and you may realize you need to buy less).
5. A simple home is prepared for the future—an easier move, a better remodel.
6. If you're accustomed to simplicity, you can travel light.

7. With less things clamoring for attention, you enjoy the things you do keep more.
8. Less clutter means less to clean and organize.
9. Items you don't need may be items you can sell.
10. Simplifying your life will help you define your style.

A simple home is something anyone can achieve, on any budget! You don't need to have a lot of money or decorating smarts to enjoy a beautiful, peaceful home infused with personal style and breathing space. All it takes is one word: simplify.

So, you agree that simplifying is a good idea, but what's holding you back?

When the interest to simplify is there, you still have hurdles to overcome before you can really transform your home.

It could be that you're not making headway because you view organizing and simplifying as the same thing. Don't equate these two! You can organize your stuff all you like, but in the end, you still have just as much clutter filling your life and your home. Organizing puts a leash on it, but doesn't make the problem go away.

If you truly want your home to breathe, then clear up the airways and get those things out of your house! The time for organization comes after. Good systems will help you maintain your hard-won ground, but they won't win that ground for you the way simplifying will.

Another thing that could be holding you back is that your approach to simplifying isn't radical enough. A lot of people *want* to live simpler lives. Decluttering is on their perpetual "to do" list—which unfortunately turns into a perpetual guilt list over time, as the clutter continues to pile up.

You might be falling into the cycle that I did time after time. January rolls around or the spring cleaning bug hits in March, and you set out with the best of intentions to declutter. You whittle away at your stuff in bits and pieces—a box here, a cabinet there. It's a temporary fix that might leave you feeling good for a time.

But if you want to see real change in your home, you've got to get a little more ruthless. You'll see the best results with a full-on, section-by-section purge. Your mindset going in has to be more radical than it's ever been before. If you look in a closet or dig through a box and ask "what can I get rid of?" you're only scratching the surface. A few things might jump out at you. You'll cart them off to Goodwill and feel like you've accomplished something. But what about the other 90% of that closet or box? There's probably *a lot* more in there that you don't need! Take the conversation deeper and reevaluate every item in your home—every book, game, sweater, serving platter, blanket, and lipstick you own.

How this book will help you simplify your home:

This handbook aims to help you be systematic and ruthless in your quest to simplify. In this book, I've divided up the home into thirty areas, thirty projects, so you can simplify piece by piece and not feel overwhelmed! For each area, I provide a process for you to follow and questions to get you thinking about your stuff. You don't have to do the projects in this book in order—feel free to jump around. To help you keep track, there's a checklist in the back of this book (page 128) that you can copy and put on your fridge or dresser. For each area of your home that you simplify, keep in mind this basic four-step process:

1. **Declutter:** Identify and purge items that don't belong.
2. **Decide:** Choose what you really need and what you're going to keep.
3. **Beautify:** Organize the stuff you decide to keep, and add finishing touches to make your space beautiful as well as functional.
4. **Maintain:** Reevaluate your stuff periodically and set a limit on new items coming into your home.

Since effective simplifying requires some reflection and goal-setting, here are a few questions to ask yourself before jumping in:

What are my top reasons for wanting to simplify? I want to simplify my possessions so I can:
_____ (travel easier, have less to clean and organize, define my priorities, etc.)

The top three areas of my home that I want to simplify are _____ (choose areas that will make the most impact on your home and stress level!)

When is a generally good time of the day or week for me to do my simplifying projects?

What are five adjectives I want to describe my home? (Not necessarily how you would describe your home *now*, but how you want to describe it.)

What are some concrete simplifying goals I can make right now? (I want to be able to fit the car in the garage, spend thirty minutes per week simplifying, simplify my attic before summer, etc.)

Bedroom

WARDROBE

I recommend starting your home simplifying journey with your own closet. There are two main reasons for this. First, it's your own personal space, and you don't need to rely or wait on other family members to get the job done. It may be more difficult to purge common areas that are shared by other family members, but your clothes are your own, and no one can (or will!) simplify your wardrobe but you! Simplifying your own stuff will get you geared up for tackling the rest of the house.

Second, simplifying your wardrobe is an exciting, rejuvenating project. You'll feel a great sense of accomplishment when your closet is cleared out, and you'll notice the results daily—every time you get dressed!

Your wardrobe is home to three main kinds of clothing:

- Items you love
- Items you tolerate
- Items you rarely or never wear

By the end of this simplifying project, you want the majority of your clothes to fall into the "love" category. Think about it: if you only keep the items you love, you'll love what you wear every day! And why not? Why not enjoy the way you look every morning, rather than putting on an item that you feel uncomfortable in or makes you look frumpy or washed out?

Make your bed the staging area for your new, pared-down wardrobe. Spread a clean sheet over your bed to protect your duvet or quilt. Everything that you decide to keep will end up on the bed. At the foot of the bed, set two large boxes or bags. One box is for "No" items that you plan to get rid of, and the other box is for "Maybe" items that need some consideration.

> *Laying It All Out*
>
> *You'll notice that in many of the chapters in this book, I recommend spreading out all of the stuff in the area that you're going to simplify. I think it helps to see all your stuff out at once, and lets you know what you're dealing with. Sometimes just seeing how much of an item you have will inspire you to simplify!*

Next, open your dresser drawers and closet, and **pull out only the items you absolutely love to wear.** Identify these items by asking the following questions:

- What pieces am I immediately drawn to?
- What clothes am I excited to wear?
- What items make me look and feel my best?
- What colors make me happy?
- What clothes earn compliments when I wear them?
- What things would I pack on a vacation?
- What articles of clothing best fit my job or current stage in life?

> ## The Packing Test
>
> *When you're going on vacation, you only bring the items you love and are the most versatile, right? Why not make that the standard for **all** of the clothes in your wardrobe? When deciding what articles of clothing to keep, give them the "packing test." Decide if each item is one you would bring on vacation. Is it comfortable? Is it cute? Is it versatile, and are you able to mix and match with it? If it passes the packing test, keep it. If it doesn't, consider if you have a good enough reason for it to go back in your wardrobe!*

You also need to evaluate whether or not each of your "love" items is in good condition. Perhaps you have good memories attached to the article of clothing, but if it's heavily worn and faded it may be time to say goodbye.

If an article of clothing is in good condition and you love it, then put it on the bed. Group your clothes by category, keeping pants and shorts together, tops in another area, dresses together, etc.

Next, **tackle the items in your closet that you simply tolerate, but don't really love.** This will probably be the largest section of your wardrobe. Look at each item with an extra-critical eye, and decide why it's in your closet. When I did this exercise with my wardrobe, I discovered lots of uncomfortable or unflattering clothes. I had been keeping them for the same (bad) reasons:

- **Because they had sentimental value**
  Example: A (faded and old) T-shirt with good memories of high school summer camp.
- **Because they were "classics" that every closet "must have"**
  Example: A (tight and scratchy) black turtleneck.
- **Because they still fit**
  Example: Lots of (stained or wrong-color) summer tops.
- **Because I was used to wearing them**
  Example: The long-sleeved (pilled and worn) brown sweater that I pulled out of the box each fall.
- **Because I had other items that served the same purpose**
  Example: The (similar to another pair) cozy, faded jeans to be lazy in or go for a hard hike.

Try on everything. Compare each item with the items that you've set aside on your bed to keep. The items that you love are your new standard, and you'll start to see that a lot of the other pieces in your wardrobe simply can't compare.

You may find some pieces of clothing that you do want to keep—perhaps you can re-imagine them and wear them in new ways. But anything that's uncomfortable, too small, too stretched out, or simply doesn't fit your personality should go in the "No" box at the foot of your bed. If you're undecided about an item or feel that you may need to keep it until you can purchase a replacement, put it in the "Maybe" box.

By now, there shouldn't be much left in your wardrobe. **Take a look at the leftover clothes—the ones you rarely or never wear.** Try each of these items on to see if they still fit, then determine if you love them enough to keep them and if there's a way you can wear them more often. Common clothing in this category includes:

- **Formal wear and party attire**
  Can you give yourself more occasions to dress up?
- **Clothing that needs repairs**
  Would a few simple alterations make the item wearable? If so, take action and try to get those repairs done (or started) within the week!
- **Items that require creativity**
  Are you not using this piece because you don't know the proper way to wear it? Ask a friend or family member what they would wear the item with, then decide if you can make it work for your wardrobe.
- **Pieces that you're not brave enough to wear**
  Maybe it's a great outfit that will energize your style, but you simply need to be bold and give it a try!

Now that your closet and dresser drawers are empty of clothes, take a look at the items on your bed. This is the wardrobe you've selected. Before hanging these items back in your closet, decide if there is anything else you can get rid of. Perhaps you have two pairs of corduroy pants, but really only need one. Maybe you have an overdose of summer tops and can eliminate a few.

The amount of clothing you decide to keep is

completely up to you, and a few months down the road you will likely discover that even this simplified version of your wardrobe is more than you need. If you really want a guideline, I've found the Rule of 10 to be a great starting point. Keep just ten of each category of clothing; ten shirts, ten pairs of pants, etc. But don't stress over the exact number of clothing items you decide to keep—you've made great progress in editing your wardrobe! In three months, go through your closet and drawers again and do a quick evaluation to see if there's anything else you can purge.

I've found that *Real Simple*'s wardrobe staples checklist (at RealSimple.com) is a great guideline for building a simple wardrobe. Are there any items on that list that you don't own, but that would make your simplified wardrobe more efficient and versatile? If so, circle those items and keep the list in your dresser drawer. If you can, set aside a little money each month and save up to buy those specific items. In your future shopping, resist the urge to buy a piece of clothing unless it's something you truly need and love, it can serve a specific purpose in your wardrobe, and it's good quality (don't buy thrift store clothes unless they're in excellent condition!).

Donate the items in the "No" box immediately (don't let them sit around for months!). Give yourself two weeks to decide on the items in the "Maybe" box. You may find that your newly-simplified wardrobe has all you need, and you don't need to supplement with any of the "Maybe" items!

Next Steps

Now that you've taken the time to simplify your wardrobe and keep only the pieces you love, Take care of your clothing so that it will last longer: Turn clothes inside-out before washing to protect the fabric and color, avoid using dryer sheets (which can coat the fabric), and tend to minor repairs, like loose buttons fallen hems, immediately.

There are also lots of little ways to make your closet prettier. Use matching wooden hangers rather than a hodgepodge of plastic and metal ones. Contain small items like tank tops in a shoebox so they stay neatly rolled. Keep something in your dresser drawers to make your clothes smell pretty, like a lavender sachet.

SHOES

Over the last year or so, my perspective on shoes has completely changed. I used to keep any pair of shoes that fit my feet, with little regard to how they fit my personality. I had lots of hand-me-down shoes that sisters or friends had given me. When I needed to buy a new pair for a certain occasion or to fill in a gap in my wardrobe, I scoured the stores for the cheapest pair I could find.

The result was that I owned lots of pairs of shoes that were uncomfortable and wore out relatively quickly because of their low quality.

Here's what I look for in a shoe now:

- Comfort
- Longevity
- Versatility
- Compatibility with the rest of my wardrobe

Do you know what's *not* on the list? Price, availability, or anything that just catches my eye. I still want to spend my money carefully and buy on sale, but I'm willing to bide my time while I save up and scout out the best pair of shoes to fit my need.

Before you simplify your shoes, **decide on your criteria for the shoes you're going to keep** (and the future pairs you'll buy). Stick to your standards and don't allow sub-par shoes to walk into your wardrobe.

After you decide on the qualifications for the shoes you

own, **think about the kind of shoes you need.** Here are four basic categories to consider, a.k.a. "The Core Four":

- Athletic (walking/running/hiking)
- Casual (flats/sandals/"around the town" shoes)
- Weather (rain boots/winter boots)
- Work (could be formal, or whatever your job requires)

Some of your shoes will fit in more than one category. If you tend towards minimalism in your simple living goals, you might find that you can get away with just one pair of shoes in each category! My husband actually owns only four pairs of shoes currently: sandals, walking shoes/sneakers, black dress shoes, and brown dress shoes that are comfortable for work, dates, or around town. I'm not a minimalist, so I have at least two pairs of shoes in each category! Here's my current shoes list:

Athletic

- **Black sneakers.** These are good for walks or hikes over rough terrain, when I don't want to mess up my nice running shoes.
- **Running shoes.** I spent money to get a good pair of running shoes with excellent support. I use these for walking or running but nothing else. I like to dress nicely each day, so I made a commitment a few years ago to not wear running shoes to the store or for anything but walking, running, and hiking.

Casual

- **Purple flats.** These are not super comfortable and are just from Payless, but they're great for adding a pop of color to a neutral outfit. Because I do wear a lot of neutrals, I get a lot of use out of these!
- **Black flat Crocs.** These have great foot support and are super comfortable and easy to clean. I love that I can wear them in place of flip flops since they're a little more stylish, but they also look cute when worn to the store and on casual outings.
- **Black ballet flats.** Another cheap pair from Payless. They're very cute and I've gotten an inordinate amount of use out of them. I'll wear these until they finish wearing out, and then probably won't replace them.
- **Blue jellies.** Yet another "fun" shoe. I might get rid of these next.

Weather

- **Water shoes.** I hardly ever wear these, but when I do need them, there's no other shoe that will do. If I'm going on an adventure like a canoe trip on Grandpa's creek, they're a must.
- **Snow boots.** This was a very necessary purchase when we lived in Michigan. If I don't use them enough in the next year or two, I may get rid of them, though.

Work

- **Tall riding-style boots.** I intentionally chose a versatile pair that can be used for weather, dress-up, or casual.
- **Black leather flats.** This is what I wear when I need black dress shoes.
- **Yellow heels.** I prefer low shoes, so this is my only pair of heels.
- **Leather sandals.** These are my go-to summer shoes for dates, weddings, and everyday outings.

I think this list is generous. I don't need three variations of black flats, but I do wear them all a lot. Still, this is clearly an area that I could stand to simplify a little more!

Once you've taken a moment to consider your qualifications for shoes and the categories of shoes you need to fill, it's time to simplify!

Decide on a space limit for the final amount of shoes you want to keep.

Do you want all of your shoes to fit in one neat row on the floor of your closet? How about in a hanging shoe organizer? Or maybe you want all of your shoes to fit on one small rack. Decide on parameters, and then work to narrow your shoe collection down to only what fits.

Get rid of shoes that don't match your clothing.

If you've already simplified your wardrobe, you might

find that some of the shoes you own match with outfits you got rid of! Those shoes should be the first to go, unless you're quite sure they'll work for an outfit you still own.

Purge ratty shoes that need to be thrown away.

Most of the shoes I initially got rid of fell into this category. Examine your shoes for worn down soles and heels, canvas pulling away from the rubber, and broken straps or clasps. **The fact that they still fit your feet is not a good enough reason to keep them.** If it's a high-quality shoe that would be worth paying money to repair, then set it aside and take it to a cobbler as soon as possible (not months down the road!).

Identify any redundant pairs of shoes you own.

Do you own multiple pairs of shoes that serve the same purpose? Keep the pair that's the most comfortable and functional, and get rid of the others. Three pairs of black heels? Two pairs of hiking boots? Keep your favorite of each; donate the others.

Pull out the pairs of shoes you never wear.

Are they worth cluttering your closet? Perhaps you never use them because they're uncomfortable, you never have occasion to wear them, or you already have a pair that does their job. Whatever the reason, if you don't wear them they are probably not worth keeping.

Now that you've hopefully gotten rid of plenty of shoes, take a look at what you have left and decide if you're satisfied with the amount and if the pairs you have will suit your wardrobe's needs. If you need to purchase any replacement shoes, make a note of that on your wardrobe checklist (see page 21).

Put the shoes you decide to keep in the designated area you decided on earlier. If you still have too many pairs to fit your space limit, decide which pairs will be on the "Watch List." Give yourself two weeks to think about it—wear them, try them with different outfits in your wardrobe, and decide if they fit your standards for a good shoe. If they don't, get rid of them!

Next Steps

Now that you've pared down your pairs, take good care of them so that they don't need to be replaced as often! It's okay for shoes to wear out over time, but they should wear out doing what they're made to do. You shouldn't wear down your nice running shoes by putting them on every time you need to go to the grocery store. Don't rough up your fancy heels by wearing them over uneven sidewalks while touring a foreign city. Wear each type of shoe for its intended purpose, unless it really is a multipurpose shoe, like a pair of boots that can be dressed up or down.

ACCESSORIES

Accessories are tricky to pare down, because the need to simplify them isn't as obvious. It's obvious you have too many clothes when you can't close your dresser drawers. It's clear you have too many shoes when they're walking all over your floor.

But accessories don't take up that much space to begin with. Belts and scarves can be rolled up tightly. Gloves and mittens can be tucked away in corners.

Accessories are also easy to hang on to because they're usually in great condition. It's difficult to get rid of things that are still pretty and that still "work."

But once you pull all of your accessories out of hiding—out of your closet and drawers and anywhere they're tucked away—you may realize that you own more than you thought you did, and certainly more than you need!

Here's how to simplify your accessories:

Spread a sheet over your bed. Pull out all your clothing accessories—scarves, gloves, handbags, hats, belts, tote bags—and spread them out. This alone might help you realize how many "extras" you really do have.

Ignore the fact that many of these items are still in great condition. That will not be one of the criteria for keeping them!

Instead, evaluate each item by these standards:

- **Your accessories should complement the outfits you own.** If you don't have any dresses that require a skinny belt, why keep it?
- **Your accessories should not be redundant.** If you have two brown purses, pick the more versatile one and donate the other.
- **Your accessories should make sense in your specific context.** If you spend the bulk of your year in warm places, you can get rid of most of your woolen mittens and scarves! Similarly, the type of work you do or the kinds of events you attend might dictate the style of your accessories.

Here are the accessories you need to evaluate:

Belts

Try to narrow them down to just one or two versatile belts that will work with most of the items in your wardrobe.

Purses

Keep just a couple of purse options that match with most of what you have in your wardrobe. Better yet, can you simplify down to just one purse? If you choose a purse in a color that can act as a neutral with the rest of your wardrobe—a navy blue, for instance—you may find that you don't need more than one handbag. If you're going with just one purse, look for a size and silhouette that's practical, not overly trendy, and can be worn for casual outings or fancier occasions.

Scarves

Look for your most versatile and high-quality scarves. Hold them up to different articles of clothing in your newly-simplified wardrobe. The more items they match with, the better! Keep the scarves with colors and patterns that punch up your outfits. Make sure you have a warm winter scarf and some transition scarves for spring and fall. And then, be sure to wear the scarves you keep! If you haven't worn a certain scarf all season, consider getting rid of it.

Gloves

I kept a heavy duty, warm winter pair that I can pull on for extra cold days or days when I want to play in the snow (not that that happens much where we currently live!) and one lighter pair that's a little more fancy.

Hats

Do you actually wear these, or have you always thought you would/should but never do? Try some of your hats on and see if they really fit your style personality. I kept a sun visor and a wide-brimmed, felt hat for dressing up.

Bags

How many tote bags do you need? Keep the one that's the most sturdy and versatile, and will best fit what you use it for. (Loading up with library books? Bringing to the classroom? Using as a carry-on for plane travel? Filling with produce from the farmers' market?). Get rid of the others, even if they're in good condition.

Next Steps

After you've simplified your accessories, make sure you have a neat, efficient way to keep them organized. Hang your purse on a hanger or wall hook rather than cramming it into a drawer. Roll scarves tightly and store in a drawer or hanging cloth shoes organizer. Keep hats from getting crushed or dusty by storing them in cloth boxes that you can keep on the top shelf of your closet or slide under the dresser.

INSIDE YOUR PURSE

This simplifying project shouldn't take you too long, but it's an important one! Having an uncluttered purse will remind you as often as you leave the house that you carry the simple living mindset with you wherever you go.

An overstuffed purse isn't classy. Your purse should be two things: **a fashion accessory** that complements your wardrobe, and **a practical item** to keep your essentials on hand. You don't need your purse to contain everything you could possibly need away from home!

If you own just one purse, you can keep it "packed" and ready to go with the essentials you need for an excursion. If you own more than one purse, **try to get into the habit of emptying your purse as soon as you're done using it for an outing.** When you walk in the door, put away all of your purse's contents immediately. Lip balm goes back in the makeup drawer, keys go in the tray, phone goes to the charging station, etc. Before you leave the house again, fill the purse you'll be using with *just* the items you'll need for that particular excursion. With this method, you'll never again forget which purse you left your keys in! Everything will have a place in your home—just not in your purse.

Here's how to quickly simplify your purse:

Gather all of your purses and handbags. Empty the

contents. If you only own one purse, separate out your essentials and put them back in your purse. Your essentials might include:

- Keys
- Card carrier
- Phone
- Lip balm
- Tissues

If you use more than one purse, put *every* item in its place around your house.

Next, throw away any trash your purse has accumulated, such as wrappers or old receipts.

Finally, walk around the house and replace any random items that have found their way into your purse.

A Note on Wallets

Guys aren't off the hook! An overstuffed wallet will strain the lining and misshape it. You'll find a simplified wallet more comfortable and easier to manage—and you won't forget what's inside! Take out used gift cards, old receipts, business cards you don't need any more (or you can file elsewhere), extra change, etc. Make it a habit to leaf through your wallet every weekend and pull out items that don't belong.

NIGHTSTAND

I've seen bedside tables become dumping grounds for junk papers, extra mugs and water glasses, old chapstick tubes, and alarm clocks that need new batteries. I'm familiar with this scene because this used to be my nightstand!

The nightstand is another small area of your home that you might not think to simplify, but it's an important one because it's one of the first things you see when you wake up and the last when you go to sleep. You can bookend your day with peace, order, and simplicity; or you can close it with chaos, spilling your water glass while you fumble through clutter to reach your alarm clock!

You can simplify your nightstand down to three categories of items:

- Reading material
- Essentials for your morning and evening routines
- Decorative item(s)

Clear everything off your nightstand (including the items on top and in any drawers or shelves), and spread it on the bed. **Choose what reading material you want to have on hand.** If you read magazines, keep only the most recent two issues of your subscription. Keep your current chapter book (*not* a whole stack of books you started and aren't going to finish!) and put the rest of the books back where they belong.

Set aside the essentials you use for your morning and evening routines. In this category, I keep tissues, a small flashlight, an alarm clock, a coaster for my drink, chap stick, and lotion. Some of these items I keep in the nightstand drawer so that the top doesn't get too crowded.

Lastly, **choose a simple decorative item to keep on your nightstand.** This is entirely optional, but I like to infuse the simplified areas of my home with a little beauty! Just don't go overboard and crowd your bedside table with unwieldy vases, fragile ceramics that could get broken during the night, or random items that don't have a home elsewhere.

Your bedside table isn't a big area, so make it part of your regular routine to keep it tidy. If you're in the habit of straightening the house for a few minutes in the evening, tend to the nightstand while you're at it. Put away knickknacks and clutter that have collected, and make sure that all of the items on your nightstand are currently in use, serve a purpose, or add beauty.

Bathroom

BATHROOM CABINETS

Bathroom cabinets are dangerous because they have doors. As with other areas of your home that you can close off, it's tempting—and all too easy—to let the clutter pile up where it's out of sight, out of mind.

Make it your goal to keep the "hidden" areas of your home as simple and chaos-free as the spaces that are opened to public view. Simplicity will work better if it's a way of life for you, not just a veneer that coats the outside of your home and habits. So grab a box, bag, or plastic tub and clean out those bathroom cabinets!

Keep your bathroom cabinets simple by cutting back on the amount of products you use and avoid stockpiling the products you do keep.

Take everything out of your bathroom cabinets. You're going to evaluate each item one by one and decide if it's something:

- You use and need to keep
- That belongs elsewhere in the house
- That can be consolidated or used up
- You need to get rid of

Let's look at each of these categories.

Things you use and need to keep

What are the essentials you must keep under the bathroom cabinet? Maybe things like toilet paper or refill items like razors, soap, and shampoo. The key here is to not keep an overabundance of these items. When your current shampoo runs out, pull out the replacement and then add it to your shopping list. Buy and store just one extra bottle, not a year's supply.

I've found that if I stockpile too much of one item, I might end up not using it or even needing it by the time I'm ready for a refill! If you want to switch products down the road, you won't be stuck with five bottles of your old shampoo to use up.

If the bathroom cabinets are too crowded, even with useful items, it will be harder to keep them neat.

Things that belong elsewhere in the house

Is there anything under the bathroom cabinet that doesn't belong there? Gather those items and redistribute them around the house. If they're under the bathroom counter because their true home is too crowded, go ahead and move them to where they belong anyway. That way, when you simplify that area you will know everything you're dealing with, rather than have more items added to the mix later.

Things that can be consolidated or used up

Are there any half-empty bottles or items that you need to use up before replacing? Keep these items in a basket in the front of the cabinet, so you can see them and remember to use them before buying new ones. Group other like items together so that you can find them easily and you won't accidentally buy more.

Things you need to get rid of

What items do you not use? Don't keep anything simply because you *think* you should—only if it's truly something you need. I got rid of most of my styling tools because I simply never used them! I like to get ready quickly in the mornings, and I was leery of long-term heat damage to my hair from blow dryers, straighteners, and curling irons. So the styling tools went out the door and I freed up lots of space!

Maybe you don't want to give up all of your tools and products, but you have doubles of some things you can get rid of. How many pairs of nail clippers do you really need? Do you need two different curling irons? Decide what can go.

Look for other clutter you can purge. I got rid of a number of random items including a broken nightlight, drain plugs that didn't actually fit our drains, a set of shower curtain hooks, storage baskets (that we had nothing to store in), and extra cosmetic bags. They weren't big items, but they did add to the general clutter, and we had no reason to keep them.

After you've sorted through the contents of your bathroom cabinets, wipe down the inside of the cabinets before replacing everything.

What should you keep on the bathroom counter?

Very little! Keeping your home's horizontal spaces clear will bring visual peace to any room. Now that you've simplified your bathroom cabinets, you should have plenty of room to store a small basket of everyday essentials inside rather than on the counter top. It's nice to have something decorative on the bathroom counter, like flowers or an essential oil diffuser. You'll need soap, obviously, so go ahead and make that pretty or decorative, too. You might decide that's all you need!

Next Steps

For anything you don't keep in a bathroom cabinet, make sure it looks good! If you keep anything on open shelving, choose the prettier items. For instance, I keep Epsom salts and Q-tips on open shelving. Rather than leaving these items in their original (not very attractive) packaging, I poured the Epsom salts into a large glass canister and put the Q-tips in a decorative tin.

MAKEUP

I like to keep a simple makeup collection and a simple makeup routine. It conserves time in the morning, and space in the bathroom.

Makeup is expensive, so I can save a lot of money by finding out which products work well for me and then sticking with them. Traveling is a breeze because I just bring my normal supplies—everything can fit into a little bag. Don't overload your makeup drawer with new items simply because they're on sale or the packaging catches your eye.

Here's how to simplify your makeup:

If you have a large bathroom counter, this can be your staging area. If you don't, gather your makeup in a box or laundry basket and take it to the kitchen counter.

First, check if you have any expired items that you need to toss. If anything is dried up or smells off, throw it away. If you have any mascara that's older than six months, discard it. Blush and foundation powder keep for a while, but toss them if you've had them for more than two years. Throw used lipstick away after two years.

One pitfall of simplifying your makeup drawer is that you might want to keep items because they were expensive or you've barely used them yet. As with any aspect of home simplification, remember that **you have permission to let go of anything you want!**

- Do not keep makeup that does not work well for your skin or coloring.
- If you've switched to more natural and green products, do not keep items that contain chemicals you're uncomfortable putting on your skin!
- Do not keep items if you don't like their texture or consistency.
- Do not keep items that didn't perform like you need them to (i.e., they wear off too soon or are hard to remove).

After you've sorted through your makeup and removed the above items, look at what you have left. **These should only include products that look good on you, that aren't expired, and that you would actually wear.** From this pile, **pick out only the items that are your must-haves**. These are the items you use every day for your basic routine. They're the essentials you pack for a trip. Take a look at this pile and decide: Could you keep *only* these items, and be all set? You might find that you can!

Personally, I looked at my "essentials" pile and decided to add a few things back in. First, I wanted more color options. So I added color variations of my favorite lip balm to the "keep" pile. I also decided that I wanted some "fancy" items for when I want to add a little more makeup. So while I don't wear eye shadow every day, I added my three eye shadows to the pile.

Lastly, there were a few products that I wanted to keep temporarily, to experiment with them and decide if I liked the color and if I would use that item. If you have products like this in your stash, keep them separate from your essentials. Over the next month, try to use each of those items a few times and decide if you like them enough to keep them.

> ### What to do with the makeup you're getting rid of
>
> Depending on the item, you may actually be able to donate your new or gently used makeup! Sometimes women's shelters accept these items. Call one in your area and see if there's anything they will take (used mascara and anything you've had to dip your finger into you should toss).

Decide if there are any extra makeup tools or cosmetic bags that you can get rid of. Before replacing the makeup and tools you've decided to keep, **take this opportunity to clean things up!** Wipe off tools and containers, wash your makeup brushes with a little white vinegar and hot water, and clean out your makeup drawer. Hopefully this purge has freed up some new real estate in your bathroom!

Next Steps

Set a new policy to buy only the products you're already familiar with and you already use. It's fine to try a new product here and there, but be careful about doing so. Don't snatch something up just because it's on sale or the packaging looks catchy.

SHOWER

A shower or bathtub should be a place where you can refresh, not feel crowded and haunted by more clutter. A clutter-free shower also means less bottles tumbling about to trip you up—and it looks neater, too.

To simplify your shower or bathtub, **you must minimize the amount of products you keep there.** Is there one shampoo and conditioner brand you can stick to? My husband and I found a natural shampoo that we both like. It smells neutral, so we don't need to each have our own products. We share one bar of natural soap, rather than keeping a rainbow of body washes, scrubs, and gels. For a good soap for men or women, try Yardley London's Oatmeal and Almond or Buttermilk bars. You can find these at Wal-Mart or Meijer. LexieNaturals.com is a family-run business which also has a great variety of soaps that work for anyone in the family.

Another thing we've eliminated from our shower is shaving cream. My husband has a can of shaving cream on the bathroom shelf to use, but I just use a little shampoo for shaving when I'm in the shower. I don't need an extra product!

Look at the items in your shower and decide if there are any that you can forgo replacing when they're used up. Do you have a plethora of sponges, loofahs, and scrub brushes? Get rid of all but the bare essentials.

If you like to create your own homemade special hair and skin treatments, like I do, **mix up just enough of a batch for one or two uses**, rather than keeping extra containers in the shower.

If you have small children, limit the amount of bath toys they have on hand. Have a couple of favorites available, and remove the rest!

Although there are all kinds of personal care products available for babies and children, they probably need even less than you! Dr. Bronner's castile soap is a great all-purpose soap that you can use on baby's skin and hair.

Next Steps

Now that your shower is neat and organized, get a better shower curtain! Ditch the chemical-seeping plastic in favor of an inexpensive cloth liner. You can launder it as needed and avoid the mildew that builds up on plastic liners. A cloth shower curtain liner is a classier way to go than plastic!

MEDICINE CABINET

It's time to take stock of what's in your medicine cabinet (or closet, as the case may be!). Pull out all your medicines and supplies. I suggest using the kitchen table as a staging area, so you have plenty of room to work.

First, sort through your medications and **set aside anything that's expired or any prescriptions you no longer use**. Some pharmacies (but not all) will accept and dispose of unused medications. If your pharmacy doesn't, destroy the typed prescription on the bottle, then disguise the drugs in coffee grounds, cat litter, or another unsavory substance and throw the drugs away in the trashcan. Don't flush them down the toilet, as this will send chemicals straight into the water supply!

We like to use natural, homemade remedies as much as possible for common ailments, so we've found that we don't actually need to keep many items in our medicine chest at all. Think about which things you use frequently, and get rid of the more esoteric items in your medicine cabinet.

Here are some of our medicine chest essentials:

- Pain killers
- Band-aids and bandages
- Cleaning ointment
- Immunity-boosters, like Emergen-C or dried elderberries to make elderberry syrup
- Decongestants

After you've decided on your essentials, **see if there's anything you can consolidate.** Do you have three different boxes of band-aids? Stack them together in one box and throw the other ones away. If you have loose items like cough drops or gauze pads floating around, collect them in mini food storage containers or Ziploc bags.

Do you have duplicates of any pieces of equipment? How many hot water bottles, thermometers, tweezers, or medicine spoons do you need? Simplify!

Make it a policy not to stockpile extra bottles or supplies. When you get close to running out of something, that's the time to replace it—no need to keep three unopened bottles of a product.

After you've simplified your supplies, set up an efficient storage system before putting everything back. If you use a closet or cabinet to store your supplies, you might want to invest in a couple of sturdy bins and organize by type (children's medications, immune-boosters, pain relief, etc.). My mother uses a lazy Susan to keep bottles on so she doesn't have to dig through a box to find what she needs.

At this point, we don't have enough supplies to warrant filling a whole shelf or closet, so we keep everything in a small rectangular plastic box.

Kitchen

KITCHEN COUNTERS

Before you begin this project, **commit yourself to treating the kitchen counters primarily as a workspace, *not* a storage zone.** The cabinets, shelves, and drawers are for storage. Try to keep the kitchen counters clean and uncluttered. Not only will this bring more breathing space to your kitchen, but you'll have a blank canvas at your disposal for creating delicious meals for your family (seriously, who wants to cook in a cluttered kitchen?).

Evaluate the residents of your kitchen counters and decide:

- What do you use the very most?
- What is too heavy to put over or under the counter?

Those should be the only two kinds of items you have out on your kitchen counter (possibly with the addition of a style element, like a gorgeous vase or fruit bowl).

After an initial evaluation of you kitchen counters, you may find there are some items you can get rid of altogether, simply because you don't use them enough or because another kitchen item can serve the same purpose.

Here are a few other things that commonly live on kitchen counters that you may be able to remove:

Coffee pot. How many people in your family drink

coffee? If only one or two, can you switch to a French press and get the coffee pot off the counter? You can keep the coffee pot in storage to pull out for a large crowd, or simply make your coffee on the stove top.

Stand mixer. Do you use it multiple times per week? It's big and takes up valuable real estate. If you only use it a couple of times per month, it may not be worth owning at all! Sell it on Craigslist.

Microwave. This is another bulky item, so see if you can get it off the counter if at all possible. We have a small fridge, so we put our microwave on top and can still access it easily. At my parents' house, my dad built a shelf above the stove to get their microwave off the counter.

Utensil crock. Once you simplify your kitchen gadgets, you might not even need one of these anymore! In our previous apartments, we've stored all our utensils in one drawer. Or current cabin doesn't have any drawers, so we do store tall items in a glass jar on the counter, and small gadgets in a basket on the shelf.

Knife block. If you simplify down to a few good knives, you can get rid of your knife block altogether. We keep our simplified knife collection on a magnetic knife strip mounted to the wall.

Spice rack. Can you consolidate items in your pantry to make space for a box of spices? For freshness, spices shouldn't be out on your counter anyway. Light can damage them, as does proximity to heat from the stove and dishwasher.

Toaster. Toasters are lightweight, so you could keep it on a shelf or in a cabinet and still pull it out easily.

Don't have enough cabinet space to store the items that used to be on your counters? That's okay—you'll be simplifying your kitchen cabinets in the next chapter!

Next Steps

As with other areas in your home, the kitchen counters should embody form as well as function. Think about how you can infuse beauty into your kitchen, whether that be with a gorgeous bowl that you can fill with fresh produce, a vase, or colored glass bottles on a windowsill. In my kitchen? I have an African violet on my windowsill that's wonderfully low-maintenance, and on a shelf I have vintage blue Mason jars filled with dried beans and lentils.

KITCHEN CABINETS

Areas in your house that you can hide behind closed doors are particularly susceptible to building up clutter, and your kitchen cabinets are no exception!

Pull everything out of the kitchen cabinets and lay them out on the table or counters. One by one, evaluate each item you have. Here are some things you might be able to get rid of:

Seldom-used small appliances. We had a miniature George Foreman grill that worked great, but we didn't need. We really only used it for grilled sandwiches and hotdogs, and even then, we preferred to make grilled sandwiches in a frying pan! The grill was also a bit of a headache to clean, so we said goodbye to it without too much consideration.

Excess mixing and serving bowls. Mixing bowls can double as serving bowls if they look nice, and you can have less to store! How many of your mixing bowls are ever in use at a given time? For most baked goods, you'll only need two good-sized mixing bowls—one for wet ingredients, and one for dry. If you're multitasking and making several dishes at once, you might want another couple medium-sized bowls. You can always use a saucepan in a pinch!

An abundance of pots and pans. You can get by without those complete cookware sets you see in the department store. If your stove is like most, it only has room for four pots and pans to be in use, anyway. Even though we both enjoy cooking, my husband and I have found that we can get by fine with just two saucepans of different sizes, a soup pot, a wok, and three skillets—cast iron, nonstick, and stainless steel.

More dishware than you need. How many people can you accommodate for a sit-down dinner? Consider keeping only that many place settings with perhaps four extra just in case you have a larger group over for a meal.

Extra sets of silverware. Keep as many sets of cutlery as you have place settings. You might have to do the dishes more often, since you will be running out of clean silverware more quickly, but the amount of dishes you do overall won't increase.

Excess glassware. Yes, glasses break, so have some extras on hand. But don't overdose on glassware! There's also no need to have special glasses for every kind of alcohol. Choose a medium-circumference wineglass to accommodate white or red wine, and maybe one other kind of glass if there's a certain alcohol you drink a lot.

Mugs. How many mugs do you need? This seems to be a problem area for many people, because mugs are such a popular gift! Even after simplifying, we have far more mugs than we need. You really only need one mug per person or place setting, right? Only keep the mugs that are meaningful to you, or that are just the perfect size for the cup of coffee or hot chocolate you like to enjoy. Remember, if you ever need more mugs, you can buy them at a thrift store for pennies!

Commuter mugs and water bottles. Keep just one per family member.

Too many containers! People tend to keep more than enough containers to ensure that they never run out. But less containers can be motivation for you to go through the leftovers! If you run out of containers in a given week, use some creative solutions like a Ziploc bag, a jar, or a glass bowl covered with a plate or plastic wrap.

Our cabin has a very tiny kitchen, so cabinet space (or open shelves, in our case) is at a premium. Simplifying our kitchen supplies has helped a lot, but we've had to implement a few other ways to maximize space, too. We hang pans from nails in the wall, and use Corelle for our everyday dishware—the pieces are thin (but durable!) and stack well. Our set of glass nesting bowls can be used for mixing bowls or serving pieces. We have a bookcase-style shelf built into the wall to keep mugs, goblets, and jars, and hooks along the top of the shelf give us an extra row of mug storage.

Now that your kitchen cabinets are less crowded, they'll be easier to keep neat and your odds of breaking something will decrease. As you put items back, keep the things that you use the most on the lower shelves. If there's a spot in your kitchen cabinet that's hard to reach, don't feel obligated to cram something back there. You've got breathing room now, so enjoy it! Your family will thank you when it comes time to putting away dishes!

UTENSIL DRAWER

It's just a little space, but it can be one of the most densely-packed places in your kitchen! Since you likely open (or *try* to open) the utensil drawer multiple times a day, it's worth giving this area some special consideration.

Take out everything from your utensil drawer(s) and spread them out on the kitchen table or counter.

Consider the duplicates you have. Five spatulas? Two sets of salad tongs? Four sets of measuring cups? How many of any of these do you use at a given time? Set aside the nicest, most durable of each and give the rest to a thrift store.

My husband and I both love to cook, and I write many recipes for my blog, but we've found that we only need one set of measuring cups and spoons. If we dirty a tool and need to use it again during our cooking session, we just rinse it out or wash it.

Knives are another area that people tend to have more of than they need. I'm so grateful that my brother-in-law saved us from requesting unnecessary knives on our wedding registry! He explained that all you really need are three—a sharp paring knife, a large Santoku knife, and a serrated bread knife. A small knife sharpener keeps them in good shape. You can fit these and a pair of kitchen shears on a magnetic knife strip on your wall!

Which gadgets are superfluous and serve no

essential function? Maybe you have a kitschy bottle opener that you got as a white elephant gift—but your can opener has a simple bottle opener on it, too. Get rid of the cute—but pointless—gadget!

Which items are too bulky for the utensil drawer and make it difficult to open? Find a different home for these items. Knives can hang on a magnetic strip on the wall, measuring cups or utensils with holes in the handle can hang from a nail or hook. You could also store small utensils, like measuring spoons, in a basket inside a kitchen cabinet.

Are there any miscellaneous small items that are cluttering up the drawer? Keep rubber bands, twisties, and matches corralled in a small dish or lidded container. Or, if you don't use them (I realized I never really need a twistie for anything!) just throw them away!

Are there any lost items hiding out in the utensil drawer that need to go home? Sort out the batteries, chap stick, trinkets and small toys and ban them from your kitchen drawers!

After you've evaluated and simplified the contents of your utensil drawer, wipe out the drawer before replacing everything. Purchase a drawer organizer if it will help you to keep things in order for the future.

DISHES

Before you jump in to simplifying this area, **consider how many people your dining table can accommodate for a meal.** If you know you have a plethora of dishes, keeping this number in mind from the beginning will give you a standard by which to simplify.

Get all your dishes where you can see them. Wash any that are currently dirty and spread everything out on the kitchen counter. Set aside as many place settings (plates, bowls, saucers, etc.) as your dining table can accommodate, plus four extra place settings.

Do you have multiple dish patterns and sets? Decide if you could live with just one pattern!

We decided to keep two dish sets. One set is our everyday ware, and one set is our fancy china that belonged to my grandmother. We got rid of our plastic dishes and another, incomplete, dish set in favor of Corelle for our everyday ware. Corelle is durable, lightweight, and stacks tightly so it saves space. Our Corelle is also in an easy-to-find pattern, so that we can add to our set as we add more people to our family.

From place settings, move on to the accessories that come with dish sets. Evaluate:

- Pitchers
- Serving platters
- Serving bowls
- Fancy serving utensils

- Vases
- Cream and sugar sets
- Salt and pepper shakers
- Butter dishes
- Seasonal/holiday dishes
- Miscellaneous pieces like a gravy boat or decanter

What can you get rid of? How many of each of these items do you need? For dish "accessories" like this, **we like to keep pieces on hand that have a simple, classic design and can be put to everyday use or paired with our china for a fancier occasion.** We found plenty of extra vases, serving bowls, platters, etc., that we decided we could live without—and you might, too!

If you get rid of an item that you later end up needing, the thrift store is your best friend. Go out and buy an extra serving platter for your party when the need actually arises! You'll only spend a dollar or two—and you won't need to feel bad if you re-donate the item after it serves its purpose.

> *A note on seasonal dishes*
>
> *If you have a nice set of holiday-specific or seasonal dishes with memories attached, you may very well want to keep them! But you may decide they aren't a necessity. There are plenty of ways to add festivity to your table besides through your place settings. A flower arrangement in holiday colors is perfect, or holiday music in the background—or even just the aromas from your own kitchen might be all you need!*

Make it your goal to simplify your dishes enough that you can keep everything out at once. Have few enough items that you can store them all in easy-to-access parts of your kitchen and try not to have any overflow that necessitates storing dishes in boxes or hard-to-reach areas.

The downside to owning less dishes is that you have to keep up with the dish washing. But that's not such a bad habit, right?

DINING ROOM

The first order of business is to clear out everything in the dining room that doesn't belong. You may need to store non-dining things in your dining room, but try not to! And if you do need to, give them their own, unobtrusive spot. For instance, if you homeschool or do office work in the dining room, keep your supplies stashed in a cabinet or small dresser so they can be out of sight when not in use.

Here are some common dining room accessories that you might be able to simplify:

Napkins. A great, cost effective alternative to paper napkins are cloth napkins, but when and if you do make the switch, ask yourself how many patterns and designs of napkins you really need. Keep just a couple of your favorite sets, with enough in each to match the amount of place settings you own.

Napkin rings. Napkin rings aren't an essential, just a nice extra! Keep a set that's versatile and will go with any meal occasion or napkin pattern. My parents have a set of hand-carved wooden animal rings. Each napkin ring is assigned to a different family member so we won't mix up our napkins between meals!

Tablecloths and table runners. Pick just a couple of your favorites to keep. Have one be a neutral color that will work for any season.

Place card holders. Maybe you can get rid of these altogether! If you host a dinner party or special occasion down the road, Pinterest has plenty of ideas for easy DIY place card holders.

Place mats. If your table doesn't need place mats to protect the surface, then this is another item you might be able to do without. If you do keep a stash of place mats, only keep as many as your table can seat.

Candles. Candles are an elegant touch for any meal—even just a weekday! But there's no need to have an overflowing assortment of shapes, sizes, and scents. Keep a simple beeswax or soy candle out on the table, and when it burns down, replace it. If you like scented candles, choose a natural fragrance—and stay away from food aromas, as those can interfere with the scents and flavors of the meal you're eating.

Candle holders. You can get rid of these if you use candles that can be burned in their own jar. If you want to burn tapers, keep just a couple of candle holders with a classic design that you can use for any occasion.

Cocktail supplies. Even if you make mixed drinks regularly, you can do without many of the fancy gizmos and equipment that people tend to collect as wedding gifts. A cocktail shaker, strainer, and a couple of barspoons are the only special equipment pieces you really need—the rest you can likely find already in your kitchen (citrus juicer, small measuring glass, etc.). Personally, we're not very scientific about our mixed drinks and just use whatever kitchen tools we have on hand!

Centerpieces. Instead of saving and storing dry centerpieces, why not use all fresh? Create very simple centerpieces according to the season—fresh flowers when they're in abundance, or fall leaves or pine cones.

If you get rid of enough dining accessories, you might find that you need less furniture to store it in, too! Or, you might at least be able to swap out bulky pieces for simpler, slimmer furniture that give the room more breathing space.

Housekeeping

CLEANING SUPPLIES

You don't need a lot of cleaners or tools in your cleaning arsenal. Certainly not as many as TV commercials and the grocery store would have you believe!

Can you corral *all* of your cleaning supplies into just one bucket? Shoot for that! Obviously the broom, vacuum cleaner, and mop are larger items that won't fit in a little bucket. And yes, if you have a large house, you may want two cleaning buckets—one for upstairs and one for downstairs. But what you likely *don't* need? A whole cleaning closet!

For us, the route to a simple cleaning arsenal was "going green." We got rid of many cleaning agents and liquids because we didn't want to have those chemicals in our house, on our skin, and in the air we breathe daily.

We've simplified our cleaning bucket down to just these items:

- **White vinegar in a spray bottle, with a few drops of lemon essential oil.** White vinegar is a great natural disinfectant. We use this mixture for cleaning the counters, toilet, bathtub, and spills and messes.
- **Baking soda in a shaker.** We keep baking soda in an old salt shaker, but a spice shaker would work as well! We use it for cleaning the bathroom and kitchen sinks.
- **Microfiber cloths.** We have five—one for dusting, one for wrapping around the Swiffer to

clean the floor, one antibacterial cloth for deep cleaning, and two window cloths for cleaning windows and mirrors. The window cloths can be used without a special glass spray, so that's one less product to keep around!

- **Scrapers.** These are for getting in corners and small spaces. We use a nylon pan scraper and an old toothbrush.
- **Cleaning sponge.** This is for wiping down the sinks and counters.
- **Paper towels.** These are kept just for cleaning the toilet and for especially dirty jobs that we don't want to use our microfiber cloths on.

We've found that most of the time, these basics are all we need! If I need a cleaner for a specific task that I don't do often, I mix something up on an as-needed basis, rather than storing it permanently.

If you want to "green" your cleaning routine, you'll likely find that you can get rid of most of the bottles and sprays currently in your cleaning arsenal.

But even if you rely on store-bought products, there are still ways to do with less. Take a look at all of your cleaning supplies and decide: instead of replacing all of these as they run out, can you buy any multipurpose solutions that will eliminate the need for so many bottles? **Buy one product that can do multiple jobs, and save some space!**

Be careful not to load up on too many cleaning cloths and tools, also. Just because they do a good job doesn't mean you need a collection. Instead of too much of a good thing, have just enough!

Too many homemade cleaners?

Just as it's all too easy to accumulate unnecessary store-bought cleaning products, you can also go overboard on homemade cleaners! Although they're frugal—even fun—to make, homemade cleaning products take up space just like their chemical-laced cousins. So keep things simple and stick with just a few cleaners, regardless of the ingredients!

LAUNDRY ROOM

If you've simplified your wardrobe, you may find that it's already a little easier to keep a simple laundry room! But if this is still a disaster zone, now is the time to get things under control.

Try to stay true to the purpose of your laundry room: doing laundry! If you must store other items in the laundry room, keep them as separate as possible from your laundry supplies. Stash non-laundry items on overhead shelves or in their own area of the room.

Evaluate your laundry supplies. Are you overrun with multiple detergents, stain removers, wrinkle shields, and other products? Simplify! We like to have just one natural detergent on hand that we can use on any of our clothes. We plan to use cloth diapers for our son, so the detergent we use is also safe for cloth diapers. With just one product, we don't have to worry about mixing up our detergents and using the wrong one! We also don't buy dryer sheets because they can cause buildup on fabric over time (and ruin the effectiveness of cloth diapers and microfiber cloths).

For cleaning, we stick to these essentials:

- A natural detergent
- A natural stain remover
- White vinegar or Oxyclean for extra cleaning or brightening power

Pick out your simple cleaning arsenal from the products you have on hand, and get rid of the unnecessary bottles and powders. You'll save lots of money over time if you can skip most of the laundry aisle when you go to the store!

Next, **decide what tools and accessories you need for your laundry routine.** This might include:

- Wool dryer balls (to speed up drying time)
- Clothespins (but not more than you can use at a given time!)
- Ironing board
- Iron
- Drying rack
- Baskets for sorting or transporting clothes (some people like to have one basket per family member)
- Trashcan

One alternative to a drying rack is to install a clothes bar or shower curtain rod and hang clothes from that that can't go through the dryer.

Setting a routine

Having a consistent laundry routine will go a long way toward keeping your physical space clear of clutter. Personally, I like the once-per-week laundry method. I don't want laundry to be an ongoing, never ending cycle! I'd rather take care of it all at once and be ready for a whole week with clean clothes.

If you decide to do a load of laundry every day, try to get it in the wash first thing in the morning—then follow through with it and get the load folded and put away. Don't let laundry sit and pile up or clean clothes will get mixed with dirty!

> *A solution for unmatched socks*
>
> *My mom knows a bit about laundry since she raised six kids! One of my favorite tips from mom is to give each person their own mesh garment bag to collect dirty socks and underwear throughout the week. Tie a different-colored shoelace to the zipper of each bag for easy identification. When laundry time comes, zip the bags and toss everything in the wash. This way, everyone's stuff will stay separate. You won't have to sort socks and underwear, and you'll be less likely to have unmatched socks to deal with!*

As you prep clothes to go in the wash, **find homes for stray items right away!** Throw away pocket trash, put loose change in your piggy bank, return small toys to the toy box. These miscellaneous items don't belong in your laundry room, and even though they're small they can add to the clutter over time.

Next Steps

Your laundry room doesn't have to be a boring, strictly business zone. If you add some elements of beauty, you might find that laundry turns into a more pleasurable task! I love the idea of adding pictures to the wall, a bright wall paper, or an attractive rug to wake things up. Whenever possible, take laundry supplies out of its original packaging and put it in something prettier. Powder detergent can go in a large glass canister with a stylish scoop. Clothespins can go in a colorful jar or a patterned cloth bag that hangs from a wall hook. If you use hangers in the laundry room, use a matching set.

LINEN CLOSET

Simplifying the linen closet is an easy, low-stress project. You are probably far less attached to your sheets and towels than you are to keepsakes and clothes. But the benefit of a simple linen closet is that it will be easier to keep neat and organized! You'll be able to open the closet and find just what you need, rather than sorting through hills of pillowcases and towels and duvet covers.

When you simplify your linen closet, do your best to stick to these two goals:

1. The linen closet is for linens. Only linens.
2. The linen closet is for linens you actually need. Not for every sheet or towel you ever acquired.

Work towards goal #1 first. Once again, your bed can act as a staging ground for your simplifying project. Spread a clean sheet over the bed. Next, remove every item in your linen closet and group them on the bed by sheets, towels, pillowcases, blankets, etc.

Have you been storing anything **other** than linens in your linen closet? If at all possible, find other homes for these items! Although there may be a few non-linens that you must store in the linen closet, these should be kept to a minimum or you risk turning your linen closet into a junk closet!

We currently live in a cabin with no closets, but in previous apartments, the only items other than sheets and towels in our linen closet were suitcases. We particularly made sure there was nothing "smelly" in the linen closet, like a dirty clothes hamper or cleaning supplies. We want our linens to smell fresh!

Find permanent homes for any random, non-linen items that may have moved in. The more you simplify your home, the less need you have to "borrow" storage space from other parts of the house.

After you've dealt with as many non-linen items as you can, work on goal #2. Figure out how many sheet and towel sets you actually need, and don't feel bad at all about getting rid of the rest!

As a guideline, two sheet sets for each regularly-used bed in the house should be sufficient. Guest beds probably only need one set. For pillows, keep one per head, plus extras for each guest your house can comfortably sleep. Keep one set of towels per family member, plus a few extras for guests and laundry days.

As far as blankets go, the number you keep depends on the climate you live in. Go ahead and get rid of any that are ratty or not the right size for the beds in your house. I would suggest keeping at least one extra throw, afghan, or blanket per bed, plus a blanket or two for the couch.

What to do with the extra linens?

We gave most of our extras away, but re-purposed a few for other uses around the house. Here are a few ways to use old linens:

- Use an old towel to clean up pet messes (or keep

as a "blankie" for your pet)
- Pillowcases can serve as dirty laundry bags for kids
- Keep a blanket in the car for picnics in the summer, or to bundle up during cold drives in the winter
- Old washcloths make good cleaning rags
- Keep a pillowcase or two to use as shoe bags for traveling

After you've pared down the items in your linen closet, wipe off the closet shelves, refold the linens and replace. I like to keep all of the items facing the same direction, with folds facing towards the back of the closet so the front has a smooth look to it.

Other options for your linen closet

You might find that your linen closet space is not being maximized as a linen closet. If linens are actually the smaller percent of what's in the closet, and you need the space for something else, then there are other ways to store your linens. Or, perhaps you're like us and don't actually have a linen closet at all!

Check Craigslist or a thrift store for a piece of furniture that you can use as linen storage, such as:

- A chest at the foot of the bed
- A hollow ottoman
- A small chest of drawers (kept inside the bedroom closet, if there's room, or in a hallway)
- A cloth-lined wicker clothes hamper
- Cloth storage boxes that can slide under the bed

Another option would be to store an extra sheet set in each individual bedroom. Set aside one dresser drawer for the sheets and a spare blanket. Extra pillows could be "stored" on beds as pillow shams, and then claimed when guests stay over and need the couch. You can keep towels under the bathroom counter, or on a freestanding shelf.

Next Steps

Find something that smells fragrant to tuck between the stacks of sheets and towels. I like to use aromatic soaps. Potpourri sashays, dried lavender, or scented candles would also be a great choice. Every month or so, quickly refold and straighten linens and remove any foreign items from the closet.

Children

KIDS' TOYS

Your kids' toys may be one of the hardest areas of your home to simplify because you might feel like you're depriving your children by having them live with less. For many of us, living simply is a skill we have to learn, but you might find it actually comes easier to your children—since they are less ingrained in their ways—than it does to you! Regardless, if you model an attitude of contentment, showing them how to steward their possessions and be intentional about what they own, you'll be giving them a gift that they can carry with them into adulthood.

Don't underestimate your child's imagination. Kids are extremely creative if we give them space to be, and having fewer toys will encourage their imaginations, not quell them.

Here are some suggestions for getting the toy level down.

Set borders for the toy realms

Create "toy zones" and limit the amount of toys your family owns to what fits within those boundaries. Designate a few shelves or bins for toys. When they overflow, it's time to simplify again.

If your children are very young, you can simplify the toys they don't play with and they likely won't ever miss them. If your children are older, you can involve them in the decision. Ask them which toys they want to give away. Show them the shelves or bins that you've designated as "toy zones" and have them add the toys they want to keep.

Keeping the toy realm neat can become part of your children's nightly routine: everything must go back on the shelf before bed, unless it's an on-going project, like a Lego set.

> *Toy Rotation*
>
> *You can keep the toy collection fresh and interesting—without spending money on new items—by using a toy rotation system. Keep a box or two of toys in storage, and every couple of months pull these items out and put other toys in storage instead. The toys that were in storage will seem fresh and new again, and you can avoid having an overabundance of toys out all at once. My mother had a policy where we could choose between Legos or Playmobile—but both bins couldn't be out in the playroom at the same time! My sister uses toy rotation with her boys, and she's also designated a "quiet time" box of items they can play with only during quiet time. This keeps those toys special, and makes quiet time something to look forward to!*

Deciding which toys to keep

Every child's toy collection is going to look different, depending on their interests, but here are a few guidelines when considering what to keep and what to purge.

Toys to Keep:

- Well-made items that younger siblings can enjoy after the older children have outgrown them
- Items your children are very attached to and request to keep
- Multiuse toys that encourage open-ended play, such as dress up clothes or building blocks (versus age-specific toys that can only do one thing)

Toys to Purge:

- McDonald's toys or other trinkets that lose their novelty
- Broken toys that can't be fixed easily
- Toys that aren't played with

Every few months, evaluate the toy collection again and decide together if there's anything that can go. If it's difficult for your child (or you!) to make decisions about which toys to purge, set aside the "maybes" for a month or two. If your child asks for them within that time frame, the toy goes back in the collection. If your child doesn't miss it, give it away when the time limit is up.

KIDS' CLOTHES

Keeping a simple wardrobe for your children will make your life easier. Ideally, there will be less laundry piling up. With less clothing options, getting dressed in the morning will take a little less time, too. You'll also save yourself some money by not buying clothing that your kids don't need.

But how many changes of clothing **do** you need per child? Is there a target number you should pare down to?

You'll have to experiment to see what works best for your family, and this will depend on the age of your kids, how rough they are on their clothing, the climate you live in, etc. However, I think the Rule of 10 (see page 21) is a helpful guideline for shirts and pants.

Here's a list of the basics you might want to keep in your child's wardrobe:

- 10 warm-weather shirts
- 10 cold-weather shirts/sweaters
- 10 pairs of pants/shorts/skirts
- 3-4 fancy/dressy outfits
- 2 summer PJ sets
- 2 winter PJ sets
- A jacket
- A coat
- At least 4 pairs of shoes (casual, fancy, summer flipflops or sandals, and snow boots if you live in a cold climate)

With less items in the closet, you can probably get away with having all your children's clothes out at once, regardless of the season. However, you might not want to if your children are the type to pull out a winter sweater in July and insist on wearing it! If that's the case, keep the off-season items packed away in a breathable container—like a cardboard box or cloth bin—and enjoy having less to store, and less to sort through when the weather changes!

Maintaining the wardrobe

The only downside to fewer clothes is that you will have to keep on top of the laundry to make sure everyone has clean clothes to wear! But it's also an opportunity to teach your children some good habits when it comes to maintaining their clothes. They can learn to keep clean clothes put away, where to put dirty clothes, and how to help with laundry tasks.

Entertainment

KEEPSAKES

This is one of the hardest areas to simplify because it's one of the most emotional. You've probably kept these items for sentimental reasons, and purging them feels like giving away a piece of your soul. If you were living overseas for a year and deciding which essentials to take with you, your keepsakes probably wouldn't make the cut. But you wouldn't want to get rid of them either!

If your childhood artwork, old photo albums, and trip souvenirs stay hidden away in boxes, you aren't doing yourself any favors. They'll contribute to the clutter in your house, and you won't enjoy them or be able to share their stories.

Still, it's a hard area to purge. I've found that one of the best ways to simplify my keepsakes is to **not** get rid of them on the first look-through. When I open a box of childhood papers or old letters, long-stored memories come flooding back. I find a few things to purge right off the bat, but mostly, I repack everything and set it aside for a few months. On the next look-through, it's easier for me to detach. I savor all the memories again, cementing them in my mind, and then I'm able to say goodbye—choosing just the best items or those that represent a certain era of my life.

How to evaluate an item's value to you

When you simplify your keepsakes, ask yourself a couple of questions as you pull out each item.

- Why does this item have value to me?

- What's the story behind it?

If you don't remember the story (and no family member can tell you) then it's a candidate for purging. If you're not particularly attached to the item, perhaps you can get rid of it or it may mean more to one of your family members than it does to you.

What to keep and what to purge

The goal with simplifying your keepsakes is to pare down your collection to the very best or most memorable items. To keep a sample of those memories, but not have every memory represented by an object.

I recently went through several boxes of old letters, papers, and childhood drawings. I decided to save out only the items that were most memorable, were particularly funny, or showed my personality in unique ways. **If I had multiple examples of one item, I saved out just one or two to represent the batch.** One thing I was very into when I was little was making "cookbooks" using construction paper and magazine clippings or drawings of food. I decided to keep a cookbook or two to represent this hobby, but I didn't need to keep the whole stack!

I also uncovered a lot of childhood drawings of the same subjects over and over again—pigs, bears, and my parents. I kept one or two drawings (usually the ones that looked like I'd taken more time and care to create) from each category, and threw the rest away.

If you have three or four boxes of childhood papers, can

you narrow it down to just one small box? Keep just a sampling, not the whole archive!

> ### Digital Memory Boxes
>
> *If you find lots of letters and drawings that you can't bear to part with, one option is to transfer them to a digital memory box. Scan the drawings or take pictures of them, store the photos on your computer, and then throw away the originals. You'll be able to enjoy the memories without storing the clutter.*

Old photographs

Our children may never have to deal with this area of clutter, but those of us who grew up before the era of digital photos certainly do! I thought that going through my old photographs would be incredibly difficult, but it was actually a pretty easy task. I purged stacks and stacks of old pictures. For one thing, my photography skills weren't stellar growing up, so there were a lot of blurry or oddly composed pictures that went straight in the trash.

I also realized that many of the memories that I thought could only be captured by a photograph actually lived on in my head just fine. I have wonderful memories of a summer camp in junior high, but I don't need a whole photo album to remember it by. I no longer stay in touch with many of the people in the pictures, and it won't mean much to show them to my children someday. So into the trash they go. One day, I can tell my kids about the great times I had at summer camp. I can show them the one or two photographs I kept from the week, and that will be enough.

Instead of filling up bookshelf space with photo albums, **I decided to store my simplified photo collection in one shoebox.** At this point, I'd rather have the shelf space. I organized the photos by trip or life season; they're easy to flip through and enjoy if I ever want to pull out the box, but they take up hardly any room.

Children's keepsakes

You might have oodles of keepsakes from your past, but you can make sure your children have less to deal with someday! Imagine if your child grew up and you handed them just one box of childhood keepsakes, and one binder of papers and notes. It would be a special gift that they could enjoy and share with their own children someday, but it wouldn't be a burden.

If you save your children's artwork and schoolwork, **go through everything at the end of the school year and choose just a couple of items to keep** (they can help decide!). Slip the items into page protectors and keep them in a binder. Their keepsake binder will keep everything tidy and organized, and set parameters for how much to save.

For toys, articles of clothing, or special knickknacks that you want to save for your children, keep just one medium-sized box per child.

Organizing your keepsakes

Before you put your keepsakes back into storage, make an inventory of what's in each box. Keep an itemized list of each box's contents in a file on your computer or on Google drive. You can also write out the list and slip it under the lid of each box. If you're looking for a particular keepsake piece down the road, you can glance at the list rather than unwrapping all of the tissue paper from carefully-packed items.

Decorating with keepsakes

One of my favorite ways to enjoy my keepsakes is to use them as home décor. Rather than buying a sculpture, vase, or figurine that has no meaning for me and is simply sold as a decoration, I pull from our own little collection of items. The things we decorate with are meaningful to us and have stories—a vase that belonged to my grandmother, a wooden elephant my great uncle carved for me, an obsidian jaguar my husband and I bought on a special trip to Mexico. These are the kinds of keepsakes we like best—some of them can serve a function, but all of them add beauty to our home.

Instead of buying ready-made decorations or wall art to fill your home, work with the story-filled items you already own. If you have limited space, you can rotate the keepsakes you have on display. Rotating out your keepsakes every once in a while will remind you of what you own, and uncovering old pieces may help you decide if they're worth hanging on to or not.

CRAFTS AND HOBBIES

Simplifying your crafts and hobbies requires brutal honesty. Your endgame is to keep only the crafts and hobbies that you're truly passionate about, that sustain your interest, and that you can actually afford to maintain. But you won't get to that point unless you ask yourself some pointed questions.

For the hobbies you haven't touched in months (or years), ask:

- Why did I start this project to begin with?
- Why haven't I finished this project/spent time with this hobby?
- Do I feel obligated to complete this?
- Is there someone else who would enjoy this project more?
- If I didn't have this project/hobby, would it free up time and space for something I enjoy more?
- What would it take for me to pick this hobby up again?

For the hobbies you invest in regularly, ask:

- Is this hobby taking up *too* much of my time?
- Is this craft/hobby beyond my budget to pursue long term?
- If I stopped doing this hobby today, would I miss it?
- Do I have more supplies/materials for this hobby than I can use in a year? In 6 months?

As you ask yourself these questions about each craft,

hobby, and project, you may discover some surprising things.

You may find that some of the hobbies you spend little time with are actually worth picking back up again. Perhaps investing in the hobby would be a better use of your time than, say, being on Facebook or watching TV.

On the other hand, **you might find that you're keeping a hobby merely out of obligation**, and that it's not something you look forward to or get excited about. Purge those projects, and purge that underlying, ongoing guilt you feel about not taking advantage of the hobby. Even if you've spent money on the hobby, if you can't see yourself ever enjoying or really using it, don't let it take up any more space in your home and your thoughts. Make room for what you *do* enjoy!

You might learn some painful truths about the hobbies and crafts you do invest in regularly. **Perhaps you are spending too much time on a hobby,** and neglecting work, family, or your other interests. **Maybe you've gone overboard with stockpiling supplies,** and you need to put a spending freeze on your hobby while you use up and enjoy the materials you already have. **You might find that you're trying to juggle too many hobbies at once,** and that you can invest your time and talents better if you choose just one or two to pursue.

> ### Supplies without a project
>
> Do you tend to accumulate craft supplies and hobby materials with no end result in mind? Try to break this habit! Don't gather supplies unless you have a specific project in mind to use them for. Walk right on by that giant sale on beads unless you know exactly what you want to make with them!

After you decide which hobbies you want to keep, it's time to say goodbye to the ones you're terminating. If you know someone else who is interested in the hobby or just starting out, they may be ecstatic to get your old supplies!

For the hobbies you decide to continue pursuing, implement a system so that you can access them easily. **You'll get more use out of your hobbies if you have a designated spot to keep them and a specific place or time to work.** You don't have to use the industry's options for storing and organizing your hobby. For hobbies or crafts with small parts, there's no need to buy a specialized case—use an old tool box or fishing tackle box instead. For other hobbies, you might want to install wall hooks or shelves. The point is to provide easy access to the hobby while also keeping things tidy so they don't clutter up your house.

Set aside some time each week or month to develop your hobby, and don't feel guilty about that part, either! Pursuing your hobbies is a great way to relax and exercise creativity.

Every few years, or when you enter a new season of life, reevaluate your hobbies and decide if you want to continue pursing them. Always keep your supply stash in check, restocking as needed but staying with the space limits you've set for yourself.

GAMES

I've seen the whole range when it comes to game collections. Some people keep an entire closet devoted to board games and card games, while others have just a small shelf. We're somewhere in the middle. We do love playing games, but our goal is to keep our collection smart and simple.

Take some time to consider each game you own, and decide if it's enough of a "family classic" to keep around.

What you might want to keep:

- **Games with high replay value.** These are games where the outcome is highly variable and unpredictable. They usually have more strategy involved.
- **Games that can be played in a variety of ways.** Keep a few complete decks of cards on hand. There are dozens of game options contained in a basic card deck! You can also get a lot of mileage out of domino sets and Scrabble tiles. Pagat.com is a good resource for card and tile game rules.
- **Your family's perennial favorites.** What games does your family return to again and again?
- **Expandable games.** You can get lots of mileage out of games that are fun to play with two people, but can also be enjoyed by a group.

What you might want to purge:

- **Games your family has outgrown.** If you own games that are geared towards young players, get rid of those as your children mature. There also may be games that your family has simply lost interest in. Make sure no one in the family minds, and then purge them!
- **Games no one is interested in learning.** If there's a complicated game that you picked up at a garage sale, don't feel bad about giving it away if no one is interested in taking the time to study up on the rules. Either look through it and decide to try it in your family's game rotation, or get rid of it. But don't keep it around for years on the off chance that somebody will one day pick it up!

When you've picked out the games you plan to get rid of, check the going rate on Amazon or eBay to see if the game is worth selling. Less generic games or games in excellent condition may have some resale value.

You might also want to just pass the game along to a friend! Your family might be tired of a particular game, but it will be brand-new to someone else.

Sharing games

If you want to add some variety to your usual game repertoire, there's no better way than to host a game night! Make some snacks or hors d'oeuvres, invite friends, and tell everyone to bring their favorite game! You can enjoy playing something new without buying a whole new game or filling up your space.

BOOKS

This is one area I thought I would never be able to simplify! My family read and collected a lot of books when I was growing up. When a bookshelf reached maximum capacity, we'd buy a new bookshelf rather than simplify the volumes we already owned.

When I got married, I brought boxes and boxes of books into our home, and my husband had several of his own to add. We had too many to fit on our bookshelves, and more than we could ever read or get use out of. I knew I needed to simplify, **but first I had to completely change the way I thought about my book collection.**

My mindset used to be that most books had inherent value and were potentially useful. I had to realize that just because a book has value doesn't mean it has value or usefulness for *me*.

Now I want my personal library to be a reflection of the way I view simple living—intentional and hand-picked for my family's particular interests, tastes, and needs. I will no longer keep a book just because it's a book! It has to add value to our life and fit our lifestyle.

Go through your books one box or shelf at a time. Handle each book and think carefully whether or not it needs to be part of your permanent collection. Set limits for your book collection. Decide "I want my books to fit on ___ number of shelves," and then work to pare down your collection to fit within those boundaries. Here are some guidelines for what books you might want to keep, and what you might want to pass on.

Books to keep:

- **High-quality copies or editions of your favorite books.** It's good to be surrounded by old friends. Keep the books that are your favorites—the ones you know you'll return to for comfort and inspiration down the road.
- **Reference books you know you'll use.** My husband is a teacher, so he keeps some academic books on hand to gather material for his lectures.
- **Quality books to build your children's library.** Yes, you can and should take advantage of your public library, but it's also nice to have a few favorite children's books on hand that your kids will fall in love with as they grow up.

Books to purge:

- **Books from college.** If you've hung on to old textbooks or required course reading, it's time to say goodbye! It might hurt to get rid of something that cost you a chunk of money, but if you're not using it for your current job or continuing education there is simply no point to keeping it. Sell them if you can. And if not, just let them go.
- **Books that you're unattached to.** Are there books you haven't actually read and can't see yourself reading in the near future? Give them away. Don't hang onto a book just because it's a classic, or a nice-looking copy, or on a subject you feel you should learn more about. Purge it. If you get the urge to read it in the future, chances are the library will have it!

- **Books you have multiples of.** Do you have the complete works of an author in one volume, but also own copies of their individual works? Unless the individual copies are very special to you, give them away and keep the complete works.
- **Books on spiritual growth or self-help that no longer apply to you.** There is certainly nothing wrong with this genre of literature, but I've discovered that these books are usually most beneficial in particular seasons of life. If the book no longer speaks to your situation, pass it on to someone else who may benefit.
- **Books you can find in the library.** The library is going to have most of what you need, most of the time! If it's not a book that you treasure, then let the library "store" it for you!

After you've decided which books you can part with, you need to get them out of the house—not stack them or pack them or procrastinate until they end up back on the shelf! **Check Amazon to see what the going rate is for each particular book.** You can search for books by ISBN. Amazon also has a seller app that lets you scan the barcode and search it using your smart phone. It's definitely the most efficient way to check prices, though it won't find the book every time - especially if it's obscure or old. If the book is worth selling, list it and see what happens. You may be surprised how well your old books sell!

For books that aren't worth selling but are in good condition, you may be able to donate spiritual books to your church library or children's books to the nursery or school library. For the rest, there's always Goodwill.

Don't forget the cookbooks!

It's easy to collect more cookbooks than you need! Consider which ones you use the most, and which are most in keeping with your family's food philosophy and lifestyle. Get rid of any that you hardly use or that cover the same ground as other cookbooks in your collection. Surprisingly, you might find that the library is a great resource for cookbooks! If you want to expand your repertoire without adding to the books on your shelf, check out some new cookbooks and pick out the recipes you want to try. If the recipe ends up being a family favorite, you can copy it into your recipe collection before returning the cookbook to the library.

I've also fallen in love with eBooks as a way to collect more recipes without taking up shelf space. I like eCookbooks so much that I teamed up with some other ladies and we wrote our own, Real Food for the Real Homemaker (realfoodcookbooks.com).

And don't forget the internet! You can find multiple recipes online for just about any dish you can think of. Use bookmarks in your web browser to easily build "bookmark cookbooks" of all your favorite recipes. To take it up another tech savvy notch, if you have devices which sync with each other, you can even store bookmarks across multiple devices so you can access your "cookbook" from your iPad, iPhone, or iPod!

While I still love having physical, hold-in-your-hands books on my shelves, my journey to simplicity in this area has also opened me up to other options for reading material. People who turn up their noses at anything but a physical copy of a book are missing out!

Here are some alternative ways to enjoy books without storing them on your shelves:

- **The library.** Get to know your librarian! They can help you get your hands on hard-to-find books, and even order books for you that the library doesn't own yet!
- **eBooks.** Newsflash: You can be a book snob and still read eBooks! eBooks are often less expensive than bound books, and there are many eBooks that aren't available in print at all.
- **Audio books.** Check your library for books on tape, and iTunes for titles that you can download to your iPod.
- **Project Gutenberg** (gutenberg.org). This is an extensive online library with thousands of free eBooks that you can read in PDF format or on your eReader.
- **Amazon** (amazon.com). Amazon offers free Kindle editions of many old books, or will have limited-time freebies on contemporary books.
- **Google Play** (play.google.com/store/books). Search for free ePub and PDF files of books by typing "Free Books" in the search bar.

If you're traveling or living overseas for a period of time, these alternative book resources come in especially handy!

Once you've declutttered your personal library, **implement a simple system for keeping your books organized.** I like to group my books by genre, and then by author within that genre. The categories are pretty broad—mysteries, classics, non-fiction, fantasy, spiritual—but this small measure of organization helps me locate a particular book quickly, rather than having to scan every shelf. As a holdover from my days as a librarian, I also like to bring a little visual peace by pulling all the books forward on the shelf so that they line up evenly.

MEDIA

In the 90s it was common practice for every family to build their own mini-library of VHS tapes, CDs, and DVDs. After just a couple of viewings, a movie payed for itself—it was worthwhile to own it rather than pay the $5 rental fee. Digital music files were new on the scene, so CDs were the way to go when you needed music.

Today, music and movies are much easier to access. **Think about the way you use media in your life *now*, and cater to that.** Get rid of your old VHS player and tapes. Pare down your DVD collection, keeping just the titles that you'll rewatch many times and want to have on hand.

Are there any movies or CDs that you've outgrown? Perhaps they were important in one season of your life, but now you have new interests. Get rid of them! Some CDs and movies may fetch a decent price on Amazon, especially if they're harder-to-find titles. If you don't want to take the time to list and sell titles individually, you can sell DVD or VHS collections by lot on Craigslist for a flat amount.

Set parameters for your movie and music collections. Once the space that you've allotted has filled up, you'll know it's time to reevaluate and purge! Although I know it's quite possible to move completely to digital storage for music, personally, I still use and love CDs. I have a CD player and listen to music on a daily basis while I work from home or do housework. However, I've simplified my collection down to just one vertical CD rack that doesn't take up much space and fits nicely into a corner. We keep our DVDs lined up on a bookshelf so they're easy to see and access.

Keep your at-home media collections lean and mean, and move most of your media storage off site! Netflix and Hulu provide hundreds of instant play movie options, and Redbox is a cheaper way to rent than the old movie rental stores. For current TV shows, you can usually go to the channel's website and watch episodes for free online a few days after they air. Make use of your local library to find TV series, movies, and books on tape for car trips.

Going forward, you can buy digital versions of music and movies which can be stored on a computer or even in the cloud and accessed from a broad range of devices instead of just your one physical DVD or CD player.

With these off-site storage options, you can enjoy extra breathing room in your home, and still have access to great music and movies!

Work

DESK

Since the desk is a work space, it tends to be a magnet for things that "need to be dealt with"—which then pile up to the point of chaos. The first step to having a simple desk space is to keep the contents minimal. And then the other side of that coin is to put a policy in place to deal with incoming items so that nothing piles up.

The top items that tend to clutter up the desk are:

- Office supplies
- Knickknacks
- Letter-writing equipment
- Files
- Mail

To simplify your desk, start by sorting everything into piles. Put all the office supplies in one pile (writing tools, paper, staples, paper clips, etc.), all of the miscellaneous knickknacks in another, all of the letter-writing equipment (envelopes, stamps, etc.) in a third, and so on.

Deal with the knickknacks first, because most of these won't belong in your desk. Decide if the knickknacks deserve a place *anywhere* in your home, or if these are just random junk items that you can summarily get rid of. If there are any knickknack items that truly beautify your desk or personalize the space, set those aside.

Look at your pile of office supplies next. Office supplies

are inherently useful, right? The thing is, **you don't need more than you need.** Perhaps you own three staplers. Can you live with just one? Or maybe you've accumulated thirty pens. But do you need that many?

Or maybe you're like I was, and you own office supplies that you don't even use! I had a little collection of binder clips that I never touched! We also had quite the stash of extra index cards and post-it notes from when my husband was in graduate school. We got rid of most of these since we need them much less frequently now.

Bottom line: Just because it's a standard office supply does not mean **you** need it!

Decide which office supplies are logical for your needs, and make sure that you don't have too many of each. Test your pens, highlighters, and sharpies and keep only what works and fits in a pen cup or a section of your desk organizer. If you run out of an item, you can restock—**there's no need to house your own office supply store!**

Organize your letter-writing equipment next. Keep standard sizes of envelopes, rather than a hodgepodge of different sizes and colors. Pick just one stationary to be your signature style. If it doesn't include pre-printed words, you can use it for nearly any occasion, whether it's a thank-you note or a letter to a friend. Keep postage stamps and address labels (if you use them) with your envelopes and stationary.

Sort through the mail currently in your desk and deal with as much as you can. For the future, keep a designated inbox for all new mail that needs to be processed. It may take some time, **but try to build up**

the habit of processing your mail each day, or at least once a week. Never put junk mail in the inbox—that can go straight in the trash!

Once you've finished sorting through the contents of your desk, put everything back neatly. Pick which ornamental or inspirational things you want to keep on your desk (because you don't want your desk to just be about boring business!). A quartz-covered rock, a framed quote, and a paperweight are my style elements of choice. But beyond that, I want to keep the space free for work!

Ultimately, your desk should be a place for creative work, not a storage zone!

PAPER

I'm always surprised by how many papers I tend to accumulate. I suppose I don't see them as taking up much space, so it's easy to let them pile up. I also found that I didn't have good systems in place for dealing with incoming paper, so lots of things tend to sit around, waiting for my attention.

You may find that you need to simplify your papers during more than one session. I certainly did! I had so many loose papers, I couldn't deal with them all in one fell swoop!

Sit down on the floor or at the kitchen table and go through your papers one stack or file folder at a time. Have three clearly labeled boxes or bins in front of you: "Recycle," "Shred" (for sensitive items), and "Keep." At the end of your session deal with the first two boxes, then put everything in the "Keep" box away in its appropriate place.

Here are some of the main paper clutter culprits I've discovered, and how to simplify them:

College/School Papers

Yes, I saved many of these! I was an English major, so paper writing was a big part of my coursework. A few years ago I decided to drastically cut back on what I saved. I threw out all of my old notes and outlines, and set aside just the major papers I'd written that I was proud of or were on topics I want to explore further. I punched holes in the papers and put them in a 3-ringed binder that I store on a bookshelf. I'm more likely to return to them if they're out on a bookshelf rather than stacked away in a forgotten box.

I also saved many of my short stories and novel chapters that I've written over the years. I have lots of writing plans for the future, and I'm saving these stories in hopes of one day picking up the loose threads.

Receipts

It seems like a good idea to keep your receipts. It seems responsible. But here's the thing—if you don't actually *do* anything with them, it's just clutter! If you use receipts for tracking the budget, or if you want to keep them on file for possible returns, then great. But if you're just keeping them because you feel like you should, then stop! Shred them!

We've set up our budget on Mint.com, which automatically tracks and categorizes all purchases made with our debit card. We don't need to save receipts from our date nights to calculate if we're staying in budget that month—we can easily check the date budget online! Most banks will also track activity in your bank account and record it online. I've mostly gotten into the habit of discarding receipts right away. If I'm buying groceries, a clothing item, or something else that may need to be returned, I keep the receipt only until I use the item.

If you do keep all your receipts, have a good system for tracking and storing them, or they'll quickly turn into clutter! Your filing system could be something as simple as keeping them in labeled, categorized envelopes. Or you could store everything digitally. Shoeboxed.com and Onereceipt.com both let you scan and store paper or digital receipts online.

Legal Documents

Obviously, you should keep things like birth certificates, social security cards, and life insurance documents forever. But sometimes it's confusing to know how long to store tax returns and bank statements. You can find how long you should keep various documents at USA.gov. Be sure to shred or burn any legal documents that you do get rid of!

Warranties and Instruction Booklets

If the warranty on an item is expired, put that warranty straight in the trash! You also don't need to keep the instruction booklets that come with every blender, toaster oven, and DVD player you buy. When you first purchase a product, take a minute to skim the manual and familiarize yourself with the features, so you can get the full benefit of the product. In the future, if you need to refer to a manual that you've thrown away, **here are three options to find a copy online:**

- Check the product's website for a copy of the manual.
- Google the name and model number of your product, plus the words "filetype:pdf" to pull up a downloadable PDF document.
- Try searching for the product on Manualsonline.com. (Note: there are a lot of ads on this site that are blended in with the content, so just be careful when you're clicking around!)

Coupons

The first order of business when you organize your coupons is to toss everything that's expired or that you know you won't use. I've simplified my life by *not* doing coupons at this stage, but my rule of thumb when I do save a coupon is to only hang on to the ones for things I'm absolutely sure that I would buy anyway! Keep your coupons sorted in an inexpensive plastic envelope case (from Wal-Mart or the Dollar Store), or in plastic baseball-card-holder sheets that you can put in a 3-ringed binder. Organize coupons by category (grocery store, clothing, restaurant, etc.).

Cards, Notes, and Letters

When I get a card or note from someone, I immediately write down the address in the back of my daily planner, and then toss the envelope. Our general rule of thumb is to keep notes or birthday and Christmas cards for a month, then toss. We like to display them on our mantelpiece or the refrigerator so we can look at them and enjoy them a few times before throwing them away. If I receive a more personal letter that I want to save, it goes in my wooden letter box on top of my dresser.

The Edges

ATTIC

Most of the stuff you have under your roof should be items you use frequently. Think very carefully before putting anything into a storage space like the attic. If you're not going to be seeing or using a particular item for most of the year, how important is it to keep?

Of course, there are some candidates that might qualify for attic storage:

- **Camping supplies.** But only keep these if you actually camp! If you're not a big camper, just borrow gear for the rare times you do decide to go camping.
- **Christmas decorations.** Make it your goal to keep these to just one or two boxes. You can enjoy a simpler Christmas season if set up and take down is quick!
- **Suitcases.** Make sure everyone in the family has the luggage they need, but get rid of excess.
- **Keepsakes.** Only save what's most important to you! For more on simplifying your keepsakes see page 83.
- **Important documents.** Organize and simplify these! For more on simplifying your paper, see the previous chapter.

On the flip side, here are some things you should consider banishing from the attic for good:

- **Books.** If they're not out of boxes and on the shelves, you're not going to see them and you're not going to read them. Do some "bookshelf

editing" throughout your house so that you don't have to store any books in the attic, and make room for the attic books that you really want to keep. For more on simplifying your books see page 95.
- **Anything that can get damaged in a non-climate-controlled environment.** There's no point in storing stuff for years that will be ruined when you finally get them out of storage.
- **Broken equipment.** Either get the broken items repaired and back into a rotation of use, or get rid of them!
- **Items that belong in a thrift store.** If your attic looks like a miniature version of the thrift store, you probably have a lot you can purge! Gather up the random baskets, clothes that fit no one in the family, furniture with no home, empty containers, duplicate kitchen equipment, and outdated electronics, and take them to the *actual* thrift store where someone else may be looking for just what you've got!
- **Furniture that doesn't have a place in your current home.** Unless it is a special piece or heirloom item, don't store it.

Since the attic is an uncomfortable place to work—and many attics are packed to the gills—I recommend simplifying it in stages or zones, not all at once!

If the temperature is conducive, you might want to stage your efforts right there in the attic. But if the temperature will be the least bit uncomfortable, take the extra step to bring boxes and items downstairs so you can go through them in a comfortable and relaxed environment.

The attic can be a graveyard for things you may never use again, simply because you can't find them later or forget they're there. **Avoid this problem by making an inventory of what's in each attic box.** Write a number, letter, or word on each box. In a Google Doc or a file on your computer, list the numbers and then inventory each item that's in the corresponding box. The contents of the box will determine how detailed you make the inventory. So for a box of Christmas ornaments, don't describe every individual ornament. But do put "Christmas Ornaments" instead of just Christmas. For a box of miscellaneous items, list each individual piece. It will take a bit of extra work, but when you need to find something later, the extra step will have been worth it!

Work through a box or two each simplifying session, numbering and taking inventory of the boxes as you finish going through them.

As you put items back up in the attic, arrange them in a logical order that will ensure you can find what you need when you need it! Keep the items you use more often near the front of the attic. If you store hobby items in the attic that you use weekly, keep those near the front. If you travel a lot, make sure the suitcases are easy to access.

Once you've simplified your attic, resist the urge to fill up the space! It's okay for the attic to simply be a holding ground for a few boxes and bags in limbo.

COAT CLOSET

Coats and outerwear tend to be bulky, so simplifying this area can have a nice impact on your home—especially if the coat closet is in a highly-trafficked area like the entryway.

Like the linen closet, coat closets tend to become magnets for random items. Pull everything out of your closet and decide if there's anything you can get rid of. You might find that you have:

- Too many umbrellas
- Seasonal items that don't get enough use for you to keep
- Ugly hats that nobody wears
- Broken game equipment
- Items that belong elsewhere in the house

For the actual coats and outerwear you keep in the closet, think about what your necessities are, based on the climate you live in, and try to pare down to the basics. Each person in the family will likely need a coat, windbreaker, nicer coat (for Sunday or formal occasions), and possibly a jacket or hoodie.

Personally, I had too many jackets! I had multiples in the same color, so I pared down to just one black, one brown, and one tan corduroy. My husband pared down all his outerwear to just a hoodie, a down coat, a Sunday coat, and a rain coat. He also has some sports jackets to wear to work.

With each of us having a minimum of four pieces of

outerwear, coat closet real estate goes fast. And if you have children in your family, the demand is even higher! Consider keeping lightweight outerwear in your bedroom closet if you need to free up more space.

Your goal with the coat closet is to have more room than you actually need. **Simplify the contents of your coat closet so you have space for guests to hang their coats up, too.** This is one of the benefits that you'll discover with an uncluttered home—it allows you to be more hospitable, since clutter can crowd out not only you, but also the people you want to invite into your home.

Make use of bins or baskets (either on the shelf above the coats, or if there is no shelf, on the floor), to corral hats, gloves, and miscellaneous items like a flashlight, ice scraper, or other things that need to be stashed in the coat closet.

ENTRYWAY

The entryway is a flux space. People—and things—are constantly passing through. The key is to keep them all from staying too long, right? The entryway gets crowded if too many people linger to chat. Similarly, when stuff eddies in the entryway the space dams up quickly—clutter begets more clutter, and more stuff will get caught instead of moving through.

Go ahead and give your entryway an initial simplification treatment, but since this is a high-traffic area, you'll have to come back to it regularly to make sure the clutter stays away.

When you simplify your home's entryway, think about how people use the space and how you can make it more convenient and efficient for them. Do people need to stash their umbrellas in the entryway? Have a spot to remove and stow shoes? Check their appearance in the mirror? Stash their keys? **Determine what furniture and items help the entryway to fulfill its purpose, and get rid of anything in the way.** Decide if there's a more apt place elsewhere for any items you wish to keep and move them to their new homes.

Entryways aren't just about function, though. They're also about form! For guests, the entryway is the first glimpse they get into your home. **It should be a welcoming space!** As with other areas you decorate, keep the decorative items simple and intentional. Don't let them get in the way of the practical elements of the space. If you designate the entryway to be a place to keep keys and outgoing mail, don't crowd the table with figurines and potted plants. Choose just a few items to make your style statement.

If your practical items are also stylish, you get bonus points. The mirror in the entryway might as well be a pretty one; the dish where you drop your keys might as well be colorful!

CAR

Sometimes the clutter in our homes follows us right out the door and into our cars, and we take it with us wherever we go! Or, sometimes we collect that clutter while we're out and about, and instead of addressing it when we get home, we leave it to stagnate in the car while we face the clutter in our homes.

If you've been tackling the projects in this book in order, the car is the final frontier! You might find that it's a pretty easy space to simplify because **most of the stuff in your car should come out.**

Gather two bags and head out to the car. One bag is your trash bag, and one bag is to collect items you need to put away. Throw away old receipts, outdated maps, items that have been heat damaged like old sunscreen or lotion bottles, food wrappers, church bulletins, and any other trash items that have taken up residence.

In the other bag, collect the non-junk items that don't belong in the car: toys, pens, extra sunglasses, water bottles, hair accessories, etc. Put those away in their proper locations around the house.

Designate a special "essentials kit" to keep in the car, and make sure that your essentials stay in the kit, rather than float around the vehicle. **Here are some things that might be worthy of a spot in your kit:**

- Flashlight
- Tire pressure gauge
- Relevant maps

- Tissues
- Paper and pencil
- First aid kit
- Car insurance information
- Coin purse with spare change

Keep the kit in an easy-to-access but out-of-the-way spot, like tucked under the passenger seat.

To keep trash from invading your car, stow a small trash bag in the pocket of the door or another accessible spot in the car. Trash that you collect while you're out and about goes immediately into the bag!

Each time you arrive home after a trip or outing, collect everything you brought with you that doesn't belong in the car and put it away. This way, you'll keep stuff from piling up in the car—and you won't lose things!

GETTING YOUR STUFF OUT THE DOOR

After you simplify each area of your home, take some time to deal with the items you're getting rid of. If you don't get your unwanted things moving out the door, you run the risk of them creeping back into your home!

Here are a few options for getting rid of the stuff you purge:

Throw Away

Some stuff is just not worth passing on to others. Throw away ratty clothing, items that are broken beyond repair, or things that have been damaged by weather or time and are no longer useful. **Put these items in the trash right away**—they don't need to sit by your door and clutter up your house any longer!

Give Away

If you have items (such as old furniture or keepsakes) that may have memories attached for other family members, check with them before donating. Give items that are in good condition to thrift stores or shelters in your area. If you donate a large amount, it may be worthwhile to get a receipt for tax purposes. **Try to get rid of all your donation items every month.**

Sell

Garage sales are an excellent way to get rid of a bunch

of stuff (and bring in good cash!) in one fell swoop. The downsides are that they're a lot of work to prepare for and you might have to price the items lower than you would like if you want to make a big dent in your clutter. You'll also have to wait for friendly temperatures to hold your sale.

Another option is to **sell your items online**. Small items such as gaming equipment, car light bulbs, machine parts, and iPods are good to sell on eBay. For books, CDs, and DVDs, you might want to start with Amazon. (For some ideas of how to sell on Amazon see page 97.) Larger items like furniture, lawn and garden equipment, TVs, and appliances do better on Craigslist. These items would be hard to ship, and people are more willing to drive to pick up larger purchases. If you plan to sell stuff online, try to get your things listed after simplifying each area of your home before you move on to the next project.

Selling on Craigslist

My dad, who is a pro when it comes to selling things on Craigslist, offered these tips for successful sales:

- *When describing an item, be as specific as possible about it. You can include some friendliness in the description to help put a potential buyer at ease—just don't ramble!*
- *Include multiple pictures of the product, shot from different angles.*
- *Take the item outside to photograph it and remove distractions from the background. It shouldn't be surrounded by other objects that aren't for sale!*
- *Don't post photos that are out of focus.*
- *Use a plain background for shooting photos, like grass or a wall. The background should also be a contrasting color, or just a white sheet, so the item stands out.*
- *For security, never put your address in the ad. Give your general location, and if people inquire and want to actually look at the item, you can give them an address and phone number, or arrange a place to meet.*
- *Don't give information about when you won't be home.*
- *Never respond to vague inquiries, like "Is the item still available?"*
- *Never meet a potential buyer in an unsafe place, or without a friend along.*
- *Never respond to a personal e-mail address given by someone. Only use the Craigslist e-mail.*

I'm sure you'll find a way to enjoy the extra cash you get from selling the stuff you purge. It's a pretty good trade-off, isn't it? You simplify your home, get paid for it, and pass on an item to someone who could use it more. Triple win!

However you choose to deal with your unwanted stuff, just make sure that it leaves your house! Every box or bag you get rid of will feel like another burden lifted.

CONCLUSION

One thing that surprised me about simplifying is that it's a journey that never truly ends—and I'm completely okay with that! The ongoing process helps me to be more intentional, to continue to refine my vision for my home and how I want to "do life."

I think you'll discover this, too. When you're finished with the projects in this book, you will love the new breathing room in your home and you won't be able to think about stuff in the same way ever again. The conversation will continue—you'll always find a little more you can simplify. But instead of feeling stressed about your stuff, you'll feel motivated. You'll be equipped to deal with that clutter instead of letting it pile up. **Little by little, you'll craft a home you love, full of beauty, simplicity, and room to breathe.**

To maintain your hard-won breathing room you might want to go through this book every year or two, keeping an eye out for things you can pare down, or items you haven't used since the last time you simplified. Here are a few things to keep in mind for maintaining simplicity in your home:

1. Beware of where clutter collects:

- Flat, horizontal surfaces
- Corners
- Closed doors and drawers
- Large pieces of furniture

2. Respect "white space" and resist the urge to fill. Get used to blank spaces on the wall, in the bathroom cabinet, on the kitchen counter, in the living room corner.

3. Don't keep something unless you know why you want to keep it. And once you decide why, make sure it's a good enough reason!

4. Remember your reasons for wanting to simplify. Whether from store sales or gifts from friends and family, you'll come across many things that you're tempted to give a place to in your home. Be vigilant! Keep that intentional mindset about the things you own, and don't let the clutter creep back in!

Going Forward

While this handbook focuses on physical spaces, as you get into the groove of simplifying you may find there are non-material things in your life that you wish to simplify, too. Your zest for a simpler life can spill over into simplifying schedules, virtual clutter, your cleaning or meal-planning routines, or your vacations. I've found that a simple home is the doorway to a simpler life all around!

ABOUT THE AUTHOR

Elsie writes at RichlyRooted.com about living abundantly! You'll find posts on simplifying, cooking from scratch, and savoring everyday aspects of homemaking. Elsie is a co-author of the cookbook *Real Food for the Real Homemaker*, but plans to publish fiction someday, too. Currently she's sinking her roots down in Alabama, where she lives in a 600 square-foot cabin with her husband, baby son, and cat, Sophie.

If you enjoyed what you read in this book, visit Elsie's blog to join her monthly email newsletter or connect via Facebook, Pinterest, Twitter, Google Plus, or Instagram.

Simple Home Checklist

- ☐ Wardrobe
- ☐ Shoes
- ☐ Accessories
- ☐ Inside Your Purse
- ☐ Nightstand
- ☐ Bathroom Cabinets
- ☐ Makeup
- ☐ Shower
- ☐ Medicine Cabinet
- ☐ Kitchen Counters
- ☐ Kitchen Cabinets
- ☐ Utensil Drawer
- ☐ Dishes
- ☐ Dining Room
- ☐ Cleaning Supplies
- ☐ Laundry Room
- ☐ Linen Closet
- ☐ Kids' Toys
- ☐ Kids' Clothes
- ☐ Keepsakes
- ☐ Crafts and Hobbies
- ☐ Games
- ☐ Books
- ☐ Media
- ☐ Desk
- ☐ Paper
- ☐ Attic
- ☐ Coat Closet
- ☐ Entryway
- ☐ Car